First World War
and Army of Occupation
War Diary
France, Belgium and Germany

2 DIVISION
3 Light Brigade
Headquarters
1 April 1919 - 14 November 1919

WO95/1374/9

The Naval & Military Press Ltd
www.nmarchive.com
Published in association with The National Archives

Published by

The Naval & Military Press Ltd

Unit 10 Ridgewood Industrial Park,

Uckfield, East Sussex,

TN22 5QE England

Tel: +44 (0) 1825 749494

www.naval-military-press.com

www.nmarchive.com

This diary has been reprinted in facsimile from the original. Any imperfections are inevitably reproduced and the quality may fall short of modern type and cartographic standards.

© **Crown Copyright**

Images reproduced by permission of The National Archives, London, England, 2015.

Contents

Document type	Place/Title	Date From	Date To
Heading	WO95/1374/9		
Heading	2 Division H.Q. 3 Light Brigade 1919 Apr-1919 Nov		
War Diary	Duren	01/04/1919	05/04/1919
War Diary	3rd Light Bde	06/04/1919	07/04/1919
War Diary	Duren	07/04/1919	08/04/1919
War Diary	Bedburg	09/04/1919	30/04/1919
Operation(al) Order(s)	5th Infantry Brigade Order No.432	03/04/1919	03/04/1919
Miscellaneous	6th Infantry Brigade Order No.432	05/04/1919	05/04/1919
Miscellaneous	6th Infantry Brigade Order No.432 Addendum No.1	05/04/1919	05/04/1919
Miscellaneous	Move Table "A" Issued With Addendum No.1 To 6th Infantry Brigade Order No.432		
Operation(al) Order(s)	3rd Light Brigade Order No.1	06/04/1919	06/04/1919
Miscellaneous	Office Routine 3rd Light Brigade Headquarters	12/04/1919	12/04/1919
Miscellaneous	3rd Light Brigade	25/04/1919	25/04/1919
Miscellaneous	3rd Light Brigade Emergency Scheme	25/04/1919	25/04/1919
Miscellaneous	3rd Light Brigade Emergency Scheme Part 1. General	25/04/1919	25/04/1919
Miscellaneous	3rd Light Brigade Emergency Scheme Part II	25/04/1919	25/04/1919
Miscellaneous	3rd Light Brigade Emergency Scheme Appendix "A"	25/04/1919	25/04/1919
Miscellaneous	3rd Light Brigade Emergency Scheme Appendix "D"	05/05/1919	05/05/1919
Miscellaneous	Table To Accompany		
Miscellaneous	3rd Light Brigade	06/06/1919	06/06/1919
War Diary	Bedburg	01/05/1919	31/05/1919
Miscellaneous	3rd Light Brigade Order No.G.S. 476 Warning Order	04/05/1919	04/05/1919
Operation(al) Order(s)	3rd Light Brigade Order No.2	05/05/1919	05/05/1919
Miscellaneous	3rd Light Brigade	21/05/1919	21/05/1919
Operation(al) Order(s)	3rd Light Brigade Order No.3	24/05/1919	24/05/1919
Miscellaneous	Movement Table Issued With 3rd Light Brigade Order No.3	24/05/1919	24/05/1919
Miscellaneous	Addendum No.1 To 3rd Light Brigade Order No.3	26/05/1919	26/05/1919
Miscellaneous	3rd Light Brigade	27/05/1919	27/05/1919
Miscellaneous	Instructions for the Inspection by the C. in C	28/05/1919	28/05/1919
War Diary	Bedburg	01/06/1919	17/06/1919
War Diary	Gill	18/06/1919	18/06/1919
War Diary	Sulz Cologne	19/06/1919	30/06/1919
Operation(al) Order(s)	3rd Light Brigade Order No.4	31/05/1919	31/05/1919
Miscellaneous	Reference March Table Attached To 3rd Light Brigade Order No.3		
Miscellaneous	Amendment No.1 To 3rd Light Brigade Order No.3	24/05/1919	24/05/1919
Miscellaneous	Movement Table Issued With Amendment No.1 To 3rd Light Brigade Order No.3	24/05/1919	24/05/1919
Miscellaneous	Addendum No.1 To 3rd Light Brigade Order No.5		
Miscellaneous	Amendment No.3 To 3rd Light Brigade Order No.5 Dated 23.6.19	23/06/1919	23/06/1919
Miscellaneous	Amendment No.2 To 3rd Light Brigade Order No.5 dated 23/6/19	26/06/1919	26/06/1919
Miscellaneous	Amendment No.1 To 3rd Light Brigade Order No.5 dated 23.6.19	23/06/1919	23/06/1919
Operation(al) Order(s)	3rd Light Brigade Order No.5	23/06/1919	23/06/1919
Miscellaneous	Movement Table Issued With 3rd Light Brigade Order No.5 Dated 23rd June.1919	23/06/1919	23/06/1919

Type	Description	Date From	Date To
War Diary	Bedburg (Germany)	01/07/1919	08/07/1919
War Diary	Benrath (Germany)	09/07/1919	31/07/1919
Operation(al) Order(s)	3rd Light Brigade Order No.6	05/07/1919	05/07/1919
Miscellaneous	Appendix "A"		
Miscellaneous	Appendix "B"		
Miscellaneous	Amendment No.1 To 3rd Light Brigade Order No.6	07/07/1919	07/07/1919
Miscellaneous	Movement Table For Mounted Personnel And Transport		
Miscellaneous	3rd Light Brigade	08/07/1919	08/07/1919
Miscellaneous	3rd Light Brigade Defence Instructions	17/07/1919	17/07/1919
Miscellaneous	Appendix "A"		
Miscellaneous	3rd Light Brigade	24/07/1919	24/07/1919
Miscellaneous	3rd Light Brigade Benrath Germany Appendix "C" Defence Scheme	24/07/1919	24/07/1919
Diagram etc	Defence Scheme Diagram Of Communications		
Miscellaneous	3rd Light Brigade	03/09/1919	03/09/1919
War Diary	Benrath	01/08/1919	31/08/1919
Miscellaneous	3rd Light Brigade	30/09/1919	30/09/1919
War Diary	Benrath Germany	01/09/1919	30/09/1919
Miscellaneous	3rd Light Brigade Amendment No.1 To 3rd Light Brigade Defence Instructions Dated 17.7.19	25/09/1919	25/09/1919
War Diary	Benrath Germany	01/09/1919	30/09/1919
Miscellaneous	Amendment No.1 To 3rd Light Brigade Defence Instructions Dated 17.7.19	25/09/1919	25/09/1919
War Diary	Benrath	01/10/1919	31/10/1919
Miscellaneous	3rd Light Brigade Administrative Instructions No.1 (To Accompany 3rd Light Brigade Order No.8)		
Operation(al) Order(s)	3rd Light Brigade Order No.8	30/10/1919	30/10/1919
Miscellaneous	Table "A" Arrangements For Relief Of Posts By French		
Miscellaneous	Table "B" Arrangements For Relief Of 1st Light Brigade By 3rd Light Brigade		
Miscellaneous	Table "C" Team Arrangements		
Miscellaneous	Amendment No.3 To 3rd Light Brigade Defence Instructions Dated 17.7.19	24/10/1919	24/10/1919
Miscellaneous	Amendment No.2 To 3rd Light Brigade Defence Instructions Dated 17.7.19	19/10/1919	19/10/1919
Miscellaneous	3rd Light Brigade	14/10/1919	14/10/1919
Miscellaneous	3rd Light Brigade Administrative Instructions No.1 (To Accompany 3rd Light Brigade Order No.7)		
Operation(al) Order(s)	3rd Light Brigade Order No.7	12/10/1919	12/10/1919
Miscellaneous	Table "A" Arrangements For Relief		
Miscellaneous	Table "B" Team Accommodation		
Miscellaneous	Table "D" March Table		
War Diary	Benrath	01/11/1919	01/11/1919
War Diary	Wald	02/11/1919	12/11/1919
War Diary	Riehl Barracks	13/11/1919	14/11/1919

woas/13u/a

2 ~~LIGHT~~ DIVISION

HQ 3 LIGHT BRIGADE

1919 APR — 1919 NOV

Army Form C. 2118.

WAR DIARY
or
INTELLIGENCE SUMMARY.
(Erase heading not required.)

3 LIGHT
HQ 8th Infantry Bde

Place	Date	Hour	Summary of Events and Information	Remarks and references to Appendices
DUREN			APRIL 1919	
	1/4/19		Settling down in new headquarters. Called on new battalion. Notified of arrival of new battalion - the 53 KRRC. Arranging billets and catering details.	
	2/4/19		Arrival of 53rd KRRC cancelled. Arrival of draft of 13 officers and 300 other ranks from 2nd KRRC for 9th London R. 4 a.m. Commander Lt. Gen. Sir A.J. GODLEY KCB, KCMG visited units of Brigade Group, and met C.O.s and 2nd in Command. Cold day.	
	3/4/19		Notified 53rd K.R.R.C. arriving to-morrow. Shoppington proceeded to new Brigade area to reconnoitre accommodation etc. Arranging billets for 53rd KRRC in BIRKESDORF. Summoned notice received during reorganisation of Light Division and orders for moves of all units concerned. (6th Inf Bde orders No 432 attached)	6th Inf Bde order No 432
	4/4/19		53rd KRRC formed Bde and billets fairly comfortable. Heads of 20th KRRC to make arrangements for their men on to meet.	

Army Form C. 2118.

WAR DIARY
or
INTELLIGENCE SUMMARY.
(Erase heading not required.)

Instructions regarding War Diaries and Intelligence Summaries are contained in F.S. Regs., Part II. and the Staff Manual respectively. Title pages will be prepared in manuscript.

Place	Date	Hour	Summary of Events and Information	Remarks and references to Appendices
DUREN	4/4/19		Reprimanded anything returns for 52nd and 53rd MKRRC who has arrived from England with not any.	
	5/4/19		Issued orders for move of units of 13th Group. (see 6th Bn Bde order No 432 addendum (Nr 1. attached) Sufficient officers in obtaining lorry transport for conveying baggage of units to station. Football match yesterday afternoon of the 2 DAC 5 goals to 1. Name of 6th Light Bde changed to 3rd Light Bde at 6 am.	
			3rd Light Bde	
3rd Light Bde	6/4/19		20th KRRC left Bde group for 1st Light Brigade, weather good. Preparations for moves.	
	7/4/19		Great difficulties in obtaining lorries to convey units to the station. Qm Inspn Regt left Bde group to join 2nd Light Bde group. 53rd KRRC left Bde group for the 1 Light Bde from Aberzhm. By 20 of KRRC 52nd KRRC C moved from	

Army Form C. 2118.

WAR DIARY
or
INTELLIGENCE SUMMARY.
(Erase heading not required.)

3rd Light Bn

Place	Date	Hour	Summary of Events and Information	Remarks and references to Appendices
DUREN	7/12/19		BIRKESDORF to billets in NORD School vacated by 5/3 KRRC. Highland Div marched into BIRKESDORF. New Commander, Capt DOWDEN, KRRC instructed march past of 52nd KRRC. Capt DOWDEN, KRRC ground to take over Centre of Bde Major. Arrangements for moves arrange on 9th and 157 Fd. L.R.E. made in morning.	3 Lgt BH de orders no.1
	8/12/19		12th R.I. Rifles left Bde Group to join 2nd Light Bde Group for 52nd KRRC left Bde Group to join 1st Light Bde Group for 18th KRRC. 5/3rd Rifle Bde moved from DERICHSWEILER and SCHLICH to new Bde area BEDBURG. 3rd Light Bde HQ moved from DUREN to BEDBURG. Fairly comfortable but very scattered. Capt DOWDEN received orders to bury his wife had died and proceeded home on 14 days special leave.	
			BEDBURG	
BEDBURG	9/12/19		No 6 Fd. Ambulance and No 4 Co Light Rlwy from arrived from east of Rhine and billeted at BLERICHEN and KASTER respectively, settling down in new area.	

Army Form C. 2118.

WAR DIARY
or
INTELLIGENCE SUMMARY.
(Erase heading not required.)

3rd Rifle Bde

Place	Date	Hour	Summary of Events and Information	Remarks and references to Appendices
BEDBURG	10/4/19		Reconnoitring new area; visits to new battalions; conference of Commanding officers to discuss training and educational work and administration of area.	
	11/4/19		The Divisional Commander / Major General Sir R D WHIGHAM KCB DSO. inspected the Brigade on billets and at Musketry. Routine. 13th RB played 53rd RB at football and beat them 4 – 2.	
	12/4/19		Half day; normal routine. Day holiday. Published Office Routine of 3rd Rifle Bde HQ (attached).	
	13/4/19		Half day. Divisional service Parade / Church	
	14/4/19		Lieut. Col. Y.O.C. inspected 51st Bn. Rifle Brigade and complimented them on their smart appearance. Spoke to young soldiers and pointed out what were required from them as part of the British Army of Occupation. Capt T. L. WARD MC left Staff (apt Supt Brigade today for demobilization.	

WAR DIARY
or
INTELLIGENCE SUMMARY

Army Form C. 2118.

Place	Date	Hour	Summary of Events and Information	Remarks and references to Appendices
BED BURG	15/4/19		G.O.C. inspected 52nd Rifle Brigade. Very smart turn out. Marched past with Colours flying. G.O.C. attended reception at Gen Plumer's house.	
	16/4/19		G.O.C. inspected 53rd Rifle Brigade. Satisfactory inspection. Raining. Capt A.W. FERGUSON proceeded on leave today. Liable to recall while remaining shown of Army Command in his movements. Major M.G.N. STOPFORD M.C. 52nd Bn. THE RIFLE BRIGADE assumed duty as acting Brigade Major of the Rifle Brigade. Reconnoitred site for rifle range near BERGHEIM. Captain Blogined arrived to assume command of 3rd Right Bde: T.M.B.	
	17/4/19		B.G.C. and C/MG Major visited site for proposed range. B.G.C., MOZ Captain, I.O.M and D.A.P.O.S. visited Battalion transport during afternoon.	
	18/4/19		Brigadier General commanding 3rd Rifle Brigade attended work conference at H.Q: 2nd Rifle Brigade.	

Army Form C. 2118.

WAR DIARY
or
INTELLIGENCE SUMMARY.
(Erase heading not required.)

Place	Date	Hour	Summary of Events and Information	Remarks and references to Appendices
BEDBURG	20.4.19		Easter Sunday. Holiday throughout the Brigade except for church parades.	
	21.4.19		Holiday. Battalions engaged in sports competitions and games.	
	22.4.19		The Brig: Commander inspected 5/3? Bn: The Rifle Brigade at BEDBURG. The turn out and general appearance of the battalion was v. good. The B.G.C. 3? Light Brigade, A/Adjutant and Staff Captain were present.	
	23.4.19		B.G.C. and A/D.A. 3? Light Brigade visited 5/2/Bn: The Rifle Brigade at training also whilst of 5/3? Bn: The Rifle Brigade and transport lines of 5/1? Bn: The Rifle Brigade during the morning.	
	24.4.19		B.G.C. visited HQ Light Division during the morning. Units training chiefly during the day.	
	25.4.19		B.G.C. proceeded on 4 days leave. Lt Colonel W. W. SEYMOUR 5/3? Bn: The Rifle Brigade assumed temporary command of the Brigade.	
	26.4.19		A wet day. Units training under their own C.Os.	
	27.4.19		Sunday. Divine Services. Lt Col. C. Seymour M.H.R.C. arrived (vice Lieut.) Col 67? Bn: The Rifle Brigade.	
	28.4.19		Pro training. Conference of Quartermasters & Supply officer at Bde: HQ.	
	29.4.19		Fine day. Units training under their own arrangements. Orders issued that no troops are to go out of their billeting area on 1st May owing to German celebrations.	

Army Form C. 2118.

WAR DIARY
or
INTELLIGENCE SUMMARY.
(Erase heading not required.)

Instructions regarding War Diaries and Intelligence Summaries are contained in F. S. Regs., Part II. and the Staff Manual respectively. Title pages will be prepared in manuscript.

Place	Date	Hour	Summary of Events and Information	Remarks and references to Appendices
BEDBURG	30.4.19		A fine day. Notification received that the G.O.C. Rifle Division will inspect 57th Bde, The Rifle Brigade at BEDBURG at 1000 Hr. 2nd May.	

Manny Snow
Lt. 6.5.19
7th Bde.

<u>S E C R E T.</u>　　　　　　　　　Copy No. 2

6th INFANTRY BRIGADE ORDER NO. 432.　　3rd April, 1919.

1. The Infantry Brigades of the Light Division are being reorganised and will be finally composed as follows :-

   5th Infantry Brigade - Brigadier General G.V. HORDERN, C.B., C.M.G.

   　　　　13th K.R.R.C.
   　　　　18th K.R.R.C.
   　　　　20th K.R.R.C.

   6th Infantry Brigade - Brigadier General H.P.B.L. KENNEDY, C.M.G., D.S.O.

   　　　　51st Rifle Brigade.
   　　　　52nd　- do -
   　　　　53rd　- do -

   99th Infantry Brigade - Brigadier General R.A.M. CURRIE, C.M.G., D.S.O.

   　　　　6th London Regt.
   　　　　9th London Regt.
   　　　　12th Royal Irish Rifles.

2. The 5th Royal Irish Regt. will become the Pioneer Battalion of the Division in place of the 20th K.R.R.C. who will join the 5th Infantry Brigade as an Infantry Battalion.

3. The above reorganization will take place in conjunction with a readjustment of the Light Division Area, which will probably be completed by about 8th April.

4. The 20th K.R.R.C. will move by rail under orders of 6th Infantry Brigade from DUREN to ZONS, where it will join 5th Infantry Brigade. Further instructions will be issued later.

5. Orders for the moves of all other units affected which will probably commence on April 7th will be issued later. Billeting parties will probably go to new areas on the 6th instant.

6. The Infantry Brigades of the Light Division will eventually be renamed as follows :-

   　　　　5th Infantry Brigade　-　1st Light Brigade.
   　　　　99th Infantry Brigade　-　2nd Light Brigade.
   　　　　6th Infantry Brigade　-　3rd Light Brigade.

   The date from which this change will take effect will be notified later.

7. Probable locations in the new area will be as under :-

   　　　　Brigade H.Q.　　　　　-　BEDBURG.
   　　　　51st Rifle Brigade　-　BEDBURG.
   　　　　52nd Rifle Brigade　-　KONIGSHOVEN.
   　　　　53rd Rifle Brigade　-　BEDBURG.
   　　　　No.4 Coy. Train　　　-　BLERICHEN.
   　　　　No.6 Field Ambulance　-　KASTER.
   　　　　157th Field Coy. R.E.　-　FRIMMERSDORF.

8. Acknowledge (units of 6th Infantry Brigade Group only).

　　　　　　　　　　　　　　　A.W. Ferguson
　　　　　　　　　　　　　　　　　Captain,

　　　　　　Brigade Major, 6th Infantry Brigade.

Distribution.

Copy No.
1. File.
2. War Diary.
3. G.O.C.
4. Brigade Major.
5. Staff Captain.
6. Bde. Signal Officer.
7. Staff Captain, Civil Duties.
8. Bde. Supply Officer.
9. 1st The King's Regt.
10. 2nd S. Staffs Regt.
11. 12th K.I. Rifles.
12. 53rd Rifle Brigade.
13. 9th London Regt.
14. 20th K.R.R.C.
15. 52nd K.R.R.C.
16. 5th Field Coy. R.E.
17. 157th Field Coy. R.E.
18. No. 3 Field Ambulance.
19. No. 4 Coy. Light Division Train.
20. 51st Rifle Brigade.
21. 52nd Rifle Brigade.
22. H.Q. Light Division "G".
23. H.Q. Light Division "Q".
24. Town Commandant, DUREN.
25. Light Division Reception Camp.

To all recipients of

    6th Infantry Brigade Order No.432.

    Reference para. 6 of 6th Infantry Brigade Order No.432.

1.   The change of name of Brigades will take effect from 6 a.m. 6th April, 1919.

                                                      A.W. Ferguson

                                                            Captain,

5.4.19.   Brigade Major, 6th Infantry Brigade.

6th INFANTRY BRIGADE.

ORDER NO. 432 - ADDENDUM NO. 1.

SECRET

5th April, 191

1. Units of 6th Infantry Brigade Group will move in accordance with attached move table "A".
   Units being transferred to another Brigade will join that Brigade on arrival at destination.

2. Arrangements for billeting parties will be notified later.

3. Instructions for moves by rail and of other Units will be notified later.

[signature]

Captain,

Brigade Major, 6th Infantry Brigade.

MOVE TABLE "A" ISSUED WITH ADDENDUM NO.1 TO 6th INFANTRY BRIGADE ORD.R NO.432.

Serial number.	Date.	Unit.	From.	To.	Means	Remarks.
1	7th inst.	9th London Regt.	DUREN	NIEDERAUSSEM (99th Inf.Bde.)	Rail	
2	-do-	53rd K.R.R.C.	DUREN (SCHOOL)	ZONS (5th Inf.Bde.)	Rail	For absorption by 20thK.R.R.C.
3	-do-	52nd K.R.R.C.	BIRKESDORF	DUREN (SCHOOL)	Road	School vacated by 53rdK.R.R.C. who will hand over all cooking utensils to 52nd K.R.R.C.
4	8th inst.	12th R.I. Rifles	ARNOLDSWEILER	STOMMELN (99th Inf.Bde.)	Rail	
5	-do-	53rd Rifle Bde.	DERICHSWEILER & SCHLICH	BEDBURG	Rail	
6	-do-	52nd K.R.R.C.	DUREN (SCHOOL)	WOERINGEN (5th Inf.Bde.)	Rail	For absorption by 13th K.R.R.C.
7	-do-	H.Q. 6th Inf.Bde.	DUREN	BEDBURG	Rail	

SECRET.

3rd LIGHT BRIGADE
ORDER NO. 1.

6th April, 1919.

1. The following moves will take place :-

    7th inst. - 157th Field Coy. R.E. from BIRGEL to FRIMMERSDORF by rail.

    9th inst. - 6th Field Ambulance from MONHEIM to KASTER by rail.

    9th inst. - No.4 Coy. Train from LANGENFELD to BLERICHEN by rail.

2. Billeting parties will be sent by units to report to the Burgomeisters Office in their respective Villages twenty four hours before move, to arrange billets.

3. Orders re entraining and detraining will be issued later.

4. Acknowledge.

[signed]
Captain,
Brigade Major, 3rd Light Brigade.

War Diary

Officer Commanding,
  51st Rifle Bde.
  52nd Rifle Bde.
  53rd Rifle Bde.
  157th Field Coy. R.E.
  6th Field Ambulance.
  No. 4 Coy. Train.
  3rd Light Bde. Signals.

OFFICE ROUTINE 3rd LIGHT BRIGADE HEADQUARTERS.

1. Now that the summer is approaching the official office hours for Officers will be from 0930 hours till 1300 hours, and from 1400 hours to 1630 hours.

2. During non official hours there will always be one Officer of the Brigade H.Q. on duty.
   This Officer will remain at Brigade H.Q. and will be responsible that the clerk on duty knows where to find him.

3. During non official hours there will be a clerk on duty in the Brigade Office whenever an Officer is not present there.

4. A night clerk will be on duty and sleep in the Brigade Office to receive messages and to take them if necessary to the Staff Captain or if that Officer is not present to the Officer on duty mentioned in para. 2.

5. During non official hours the clerk on duty will take all telegrams which arrive between 0930 and 2200 hours at once to an Officer.
   Between 2200 and 0930 hours as a general rule only "Priority" telegrams and letters marked urgent will be so taken, but the clerk on duty must use his discretion should other telegrams etc. arrive which appear to require immediate action.

6. Saturday will normally be treated as a half holiday, and Sunday as a "dies non" but from 1300 hours on Saturday till 0930 hours on Monday the arrangements indicated in paras. 2,3,4 and 5 above will remain in force.

7. The general principle will be that no message of an urgent nature can arrive at any hour of the day or night without receiving immediate attention.

8. The above arrangements will come into force from 1300 hours 13th inst.

                    (sgd) A.W. FERGUSON,
                              Captain,

12.4.19.   Brigade Major, 3rd Light Brigade.

3RD. LIGHT BRIGADE.

BEDBURG.   April 25th, 1919.

Herewith Parts 1 & 11 of 3rd Light Brigade Emergency Scheme

Copy No __18__.   Also Appendices A, B, C.

Appendix "D" and Map will follow.

Acknowledge

J.K. Newbagging.
Captain for Major,
A/Brigade Major, 3rd. Light Bde.

25/4/'19.

3RD. LIGHT BRIGADE.

EMERGENCY SCHEME.

SECRET
25/4/19

CONTENTS.

Part 1.   GENERAL.

Part 11   Action to be taken in the event of Civil
                disturbances or emergency within the areas
                occupied by Units of the 3rd. Light Brigade
                Group.

Appendix "A"   Composition of 3rd. Light Brigade Group.

Appendix "B"   Disposal of Surplus Baggage and Guards.

Appendix "C"   General Instructions for entraining

Appendix "D"   Scheme for BEDBURG.

Map 1. to accompany Appendix "D"

3RD. LIGHT BRIGADE.

25/4/19

"EMERGENCY SCHEME"

PART 1. GENERAL.

1. The following scheme is issued to meet the contingency of the Brigade Group, or a portion of the Brigade, being suddenly required to move to deal with Civil disturbances or other emergency.

2. As it is not possible to tell in what direction the Brigade Group might be required to act, it must be prepared to move in any direction. This scheme is therefore divided into two parts - Part 1 deals with general points which would affect a move in any direction; Part 11 deals with the action to be taken in the event of civil disturbances in the villages in which Units are at present located.

3. ### Composition of 3rd Light Brigade Group.

   The composition of the 3rd. Light Brigade Group and the location of Units is given in Appendix "A". In the event of a move being ordered, a proportion, depending on the requirements of the situation, of the Divisional Artillery, Machine Gun and Pioneer Battalions would probably be allotted to the Brigade.

4. ### Descriptions of Battalions.

   For the purposes of this scheme, Battalions will be known by the following names:-

   (a) The Battalion billeted in the SCHLOSS and the east end of BEDBURG - - - "SCHLOSS BN.
   (b) The Battalion billeted in the LINOLEUM Factory - - "LINOLEUM BN.
   (c) The Battalion at KONIGSHOVEN - KONIGSHOVEN BN.

5. ### Warning Order

   As soon as it is apparent that the move of the Brigade Group or a portion of the Group, is imminent, the code-word "MOBILE" will be sent from Brigade Headquarters by wire. This will mean that the Units to whom the message is addressed will get ready to move. If only certain Units are required to be in readiness, the name of the Units concerned will precede the code-word, e.g. The Battalion at KONIGSHOVEN and the 3rd. Light Brigade Trench Mortar Battery - - - "KONIGSHOVEN BN. and 3RD L.T.M.B. MOBILE.

6. ### Action on receipt of Warning Order

   On receipt of the warning order, the following action will be taken:-

   (a) Units concerned will collect all men away from Billets, and prepare to move at half-an-hour's notice.
   (b) Water Bottles and Water Carts will be filled.
   (c) Ammunition will be issued to complete to 120 rounds S.A.A. per man, except Lewis Gun Teams, (vide Paragraph 8)

25/4/19

(d) 20 Drums per Lewis Gun will be filled.
(e) One box of Bombs per platoon will be detonated and carried on Regimental Transport.
(f) Surplus Kits and blankets will be stacked under Unit arrangements, and left in charge of a guard. (Vide Appendix "B")
(g) Baggage-Wagons will join Units. Supply wagons will be dealt with under orders issued by Brigade Headquarters, according to the supply situation at the time the warning order is issued.
(h) Transport will be loaded and horses harnessed but not hooked in.
(k) All Units will send an Officer (Mounted or on a Bicycle) and an orderly to report at Brigade Headquarters.
(l) Battalions will be organised in accordance with O.B. 1919 of Sept. 1918, paras 1, 2, and 3.
The personnel detailed in O.B.1919 of Sept 1918 will be left behind in the Unit Billeting Area and will be utilized to provide guards over Kits and stores left behind, and such other duties as may be necessary. Sick will be disposed of in accordance with instructions to be issued later.
The name of the Senior Officer i/c the details of each Battalion will be reported to Brigade Headquarters.
These details will be provided with the unconsumed portion of the day's Rations and Rations for the following day.

Para 7 on separate sheet

8. Orders to Move.

(a) For the present, Infantry will move in Marching Order, i.e. wearing Steel Helmets and carrying packs and Great Coats.
(b) The following will be carried on the man:-
   (i) 120 Rounds S.A.A. per man, except Lewis Gun Teams, which will carry 50 Rounds per man.
   (ii) Unexpended portion of the day's Rations. Separate instructions will be issued as to Iron Rations.
(c) Bombs, vide Paragraph 9.
(d) Personnel of other units will wear Marching Order.

9. Bombs and Rifle Grenades.

(a) In the event of Civil Disturbances, bombs would probably be required to drive parties out of houses and cellars. Eight men per platoon (2 per section including L.G.Section) will be specially trained to detonate and use bombs and Rifle Grenades.
(b) No Bombs or Rifle grenades will normally be carried on the man during the march to the area of operations. Arrangements will, however, be made so that bombs and Rifle Grenades can be issued to, and detonated by, the eight selected men per platoon (vide paragraph 9 (a)) before moving off from the Battalion assembly positions, if required.
(c) Bombs and Rifle Grenades carried on Regimental Transport, with the exception of one box of bombs per platoon, will not be detonated.

10. 3rd. Light Brigade T.M.B.
The 3rd. Light Brigade Lt.Trench Mortar Battery will move with 3 Guns and 298 bombs. Bombs will not be carried detonated during the march to the area of operations, but arrangements will be made so that they can be detonated quickly, if required, before moving off from the assembly position.

3rd Light Brigade Emergency Scheme. 25/4/'19

Part 1. (Con)

Order to move.

7.

(a) The order for Units to move to any Rendez-vous or area will be wired in clear from Brigade Headquarters, giving sufficient detail for troops to commence their move in the required direction.

Further Orders as to the situation and roles of the various Units will follow.

(b) As, in certain contingencies, troops may be required to move by rail, all Units composing the Brigade Group will reconnoitre HARFF and BEDBURG RAILWAY STATIONS with a view to entraining. Special attention will be paid to the facilities at these Stations for entraining Horses and Transport Vehicles.

General instructions with regard to entraining are given in Appendix "C"

11. **Garrison.**

In the event of certain Units only of the Brigade Group being required to move, the areas vacated by them will be garrisoned by detachments from other Units on receipt of instructions from Brigade Headquarters. The strength of these garrisons will depend on the requirements of the movement, but each Battalion must be prepared to provide at least one Company for this duty.

12. **Field Company. R.E.**

Composition and strength of Field Companys will be decided by the C.R.E., and in the event of this scheme taking effect the O.C. Field Coy. will at once notify Brigade Headquarters what this will be

13. **Field Ambulance**

Arrangements in connection with the Field Ambulance will be notified later.

14. **D.A.C.**

In the event of the Brigade Group moving independently or being detached from the Division, one section of the S.A.A. Section, Light Division D.A.C., will be placed under the orders of the B.G.C. 3rd. Light Brigade, upon receipt of instructions from Divisional Headquarters.

15. **Details at Divisional H.Q.**

Should the whole Division be ordered to move to deal with a a sudden emergency, the following details will not move with the Division in the first instance, but will be concentrated in BEDBURG under orders to be issued by Divisional H.Q.:-

Employment Company.
Reception Camp.
Laundry.
Canteen.
D.A.D.O.S. Stores.

16. **Cadres.**

2nd. Division Cadres will remain in their present locations and take the necessary steps for their local protection.

17.

O.C. Units will draw up detailed schemes on the foregoing basis with a view to the rapid execution of a sudden move if one is ordered.

Major,

A/Brigade Major, 3rd. Light Brigade.

3RD. LIGHT BRIGADE.

EMERGENCY SCHEME.

PART II.

Action to be taken in the event of civil
disturbances or emergency within the areas
occupied by units of 3rd. Light Brigade Group.

1. In the event of civil disturbances or other emergencies within the area occupied by units of the Brigade Group, the general policy to be adopted is that each unit will be responsible for the safety of the area within which it is billeted.

2. **GENERAL PRINCIPLES.**

    In order that this policy may be carried out, the following principles will be adhered to:-

    (a) Picquets will be posted on all roads leading into villages, to prevent the ingress or egress of all unauthorized persons.

    (b) Guards will be mounted on bridges, factories, water works, railway stations and other buildings of importance within the unit's billeting area.

    (c) Armed patrols under an officer will move through villages to maintain order.

3. **METHOD OF REPORTING DISTURBANCES.**

    (a) In the event of disturbances arising, the unit in whose area the disturbance takes place will wire the code-word "ALARM" followed by the name of the village affected, to Brigade Headquarters; e.g. "ALARM KONIGSHOVEN". This message will be repeated from Brigade Headquarters to Divisional Headquarters, and will be supplemented as early as possible by a telegraphic report stating the nature and extent of the disturbance.

    (b) In the event of disturbances arising in BEDBURG, the code message will be wired to Brigade Headquarters, and repeated to other units in the village, by the unit first noticing signs of the disturbance. The "ALARM" will be sounded and taken up by all buglers in the village.

    (c) If the disturbances appear to be of a serious nature and assistance is likely to be required from troops outside the area affected, the "MOBILE" message (vide EMERGENCY SCHEME PART I, paragraph 5) will be issued from Brigade Headquarters.

- 2 -

25/4/19

4. ACTION TO BE TAKEN ON RECEIPT OF OR ISSUE OF ALARM MESSAGE.

As soon as any disturbance arises or the "ALARM" message is received, the following action will be taken by units concerned:-

(a) Units will fall in on their alarm posts with steel helmets, arms and ammunition.

(b) The picquets, guards and patrols mentioned in paragraph 2 above, will take up their positions.

(c) Double sentries will be posted on all billets.

(d) Guards on ammunition and ration stores will be doubled.

(e) Civilians will be confined to their houses.

(f) After dark all street-lamps and lights in houses will be lit, blinds drawn up and shutters opened, so that any movements in the streets may be observed.

5. COMMUNICATION.

In view of the possibility of telegraph wires being destroyed, the Brigade Signalling Officer will prepare a scheme for visual communication between Brigade Headquarters and outlying units.

6. Commanding Officers will draw up detailed schemes, based on the foregoing, for the protection of their billeting areas. The scheme for BEDBURG will be drawn up at Brigade Headquarters and issued as Appendix "D".

Major,
Acting Brigade-Major,
3rd. Light Brigade.

25/4/19

3rd. LIGHT BRIGADE.

EMERGENCY SCHEME.

APPENDIX "A"

COMPOSITION OF 3RD LIGHT BRIGADE GROUP.

Headquarters 3rd Light Brigade.	BEDBURG. (Burgomaster's Office)
51st. Bn. The Rifle Brigade.	BEDBURG.
52nd. Bn. The Rifle Brigade.	KONIGSHOVEN.
53rd. Bn. The Rifle Brigade.	BEDBURG.
3rd. Light Bde. T.M.Battery.	MILLENDORF.
157th. Field Company R.E.	BUCHHOLZ
No.3 Field Ambulance.	KASTER.
No. 4 Company Light Divisional Train.	BLERICHEN.

3RD. LIGHT BRIGADE.

BEDBURG, Germany.   EMERGENCY SCHEME   5th. May 1919.

COPY NO. 15

APPENDIX "D".

SCHEME FOR BEDBURG AND BLERICHEN.

REFERENCE MAP I ATTACHED. *Map issued only to 51st & 53rd Bde*

1. In the event of civil disturbances or other emergency in BEDBURG or BLERICHEN, the instructions laid down in Part II will be carried out automatically by units.

2. AREAS OF RESPONSIBILITY.

    The areas of responsibility for Battalions are shown on Map I attached.

3. LIGHT DIVISION M.T. COMPANY.

    The Light Division M.T. Company will be responsible for the protection and safety of their own lorries.

4. INLYING PICQUETS.

    On the alarm being given, inlying picquets will fall in at once on unit alarm posts, after which their subsequent employment will be ordered from Brigade Headquarters.

5. GUARDS, PICQUETS AND PATROLS.

    The positions for and approximate strength of the guards, picquets and patrols to be found by units are shown on the TABLE overleaf. These will not be found from the Company on inlying picquet.
    (a) Guards will be responsible for the protection and safety of the place over which they are mounted.
    (b) Picquets will prevent any civilians from entering or leaving the village. In case of doubt as to whether a civilian may enter or leave the village, he will be sent under escort to Brigade Headquarters.
    (c) Patrols will see that all civilians remain in their houses, and that the instructions contained in Part II, paragraph 4 (f), are carried out after dark.

6. CIVILIANS.

    Any suspected persons or civilians who fail to carry out the orders given to them will be arrested.

7. Officers Commanding Units will draw up schemes based on the foregoing. Personnel for guards, picquets and patrols will be earmarked and will be practiced in taking up their positions.

TABLE TO ACCOMPANY.
****

UNIT.	PICQUETS.		GUARDS.		PATROLS.		REMARKS.
	At.	Strength.	At.	Strength.	Route.	Strength.	
chloss Bn.	"A"	1 Section.	Electricity Works.	1 N.C.O. 6 men.	All roads within Battalion "Area of Responsibil-ity".		All guards will be in addition to those normally found by Units.
	"B"	1 Platoon.	Sugar Fcty.	1 Platoon.		All parades will invari--ably be under an officer, and will be not less in strength than 2 sections, or more than 1 platoon.	
	"C"	1 L.G.Sectn.					
	"D"	1 Section.	Bde. H.Q.	1 N.C.O. 6 men.			
	"E"	1 Section.	Bde. Q.M. Stores.	1 N.C.O. 6 men.			
	"F"	1 Section.					
	"G"	Double Sentry.	Bde. Signal Office.	1 N.C.O. 6 men.			
	"H"	Double Sentry.					
	"K"	1 L.G.Sectn.	Brickworks.	1 Section.			
	"Y"	1 L.G.Sectn.	Wool-Factory Linoleum Wks. (Station Bldgs. (&Level Crossg. (Div. Canteen (Store. Y.M.C.A.	1 Platoon. Bn. ½ Guard 1 Platoon. 1 N.C.O. 6 men. 1 N.C.O. 6 men.	All roads within Battn. "Area of Responsibil-ity".		
NOLEUM ttn.	"Z"	(1 L.G.Sectn (& 1 Section.	Engine House.	1 N.C.O. 6 men.			

3rd LIGHT BRIGADE.
****

BEDBURG, Germany.

6th June, 1919.

HEADQUARTERS, 3RD LIGHT BRIGADE.

Herewith duplicate War Diaries with appendices of 3rd Light Brigade H.Q. for months of April and May 1919.

Please acknowledge receipt.

W. D. Seymour.

Lieut-Colonel,
Commanding, 3rd Light Brigade.

The Secretary,
   War Office,
      LONDON.

The Secretary
   War Office London

Herewith Duplicate War Diaries of
3rd Light Brigade for months of
April and May 1919

                              Lt Col

Army Form C. 2118.

WAR DIARY
or
INTELLIGENCE SUMMARY.
(Erase heading not required.)

HEADQUARTERS, 3RD. LIGHT BRIGADE.

MAY 1919.

Instructions regarding War Diaries and Intelligence Summaries are contained in F. S. Regs., Part II. and the Staff Manual respectively. Title pages will be prepared in manuscript.

Place	Date	Hour	Summary of Events and Information	Remarks and references to Appendices
BEDBURG	1-5-19.		All troops confined to their unit billetting areas for the day, owing to German celebrations. Civilians in the Brigade Area quiet and had no demonstrations. A wet day.	
	2-5-19.		Capt. C.H. DOWDEN returned from leave and assumed duties of Brigade Major, 3rd. Light Brigade.	
	3-5-19.		Training, Education and Parades as usual.	
	4-5-19.		Sunday - Church parades.	
	5-5-19.		Training and Education.	
	6-5-19.		H.R.H. Field Marshal, The Duke of Connaught inspected the Brigade. The Brigade was drawn up on parade and received H.R.H. with a Royal Salute. H.R.H. walked round all Battalions, and, on conclusion, addressed the Brigade. H.R.H. then led the Brigade in three cheers for H.M. The King. After giving three cheers for H.R.H. The Duke, the Brigade marched past in column of route. Both the Corps and Divisional Commanders were in attendance. 3rd. Light Brigade Order No. 2.	App. No.1.
	7-5-19.		The usual Training and Education carried out under battalion arrangements.	
	8-5-19.		Training and Education - Lecture to 53rd. Rifle Brigade by Canon Meyrick in Y.M.C.A. at 1030 hours. Subject - Reconstruction.	
	9-5-19.		51st. Bn. weekly route-march: others usual training. Staff Captain proceeded on leave.	
	10-5-19.		Orders received that Cadres of 1st. King's, 2nd. S. Staffs., 10th. D.C.L.I. and 5th. Field Company, would be moved from East of the Rhine to BUIR, and come under 3rd. Light Brigade on arrival. Billets arranged at BUIR. The usual Training and Education carried out. Major Stopford arrived from leave and took over duties of Staff Captain.	
	11-5-19.		Sunday - Church parades. Cadres arrived at BUIR about 1500 - 1600 hours.	

Army Form C. 2118.

WAR DIARY
or
INTELLIGENCE SUMMARY.
(Erase heading not required.)

Instructions regarding War Diaries and Intelligence Summaries are contained in F.S. Regs., Part II. and the Staff Manual respectively. Title pages will be prepared in manuscript.

Place	Date	Hour	Summary of Events and Information	Remarks and references to Appendices
BEDBURG.	12-5-19.		Inspection of 3rd. Light Trench Mortar Battery by the Brigadier, at 1050 hours. Lecture by Mr. HAYWARD on Citizenship to 52nd. Rifle Brigade, at 1100 hours. Education and Training as usual.	
	13-5-19.		Lectures, Training and Education as usual.	
	14-5-19.		Training as usual.	
	15-5-19.		Training and Education.	
	16-5-19.		Usual platoon and company training, all units firing on 50 yds. range. Education for all ranks and lectures.	
	17-5-19.		Training as for 16th. instant.	
	18-5-19.		Church Parades.	
	19-5-19.		Training and Education. Conference of C.Os. at 1150 hours.	
	20-5-19.		Usual Training and Education.	
	21-5-19.		Training as usual.	
	22-5-19.		Instructions issued by Division as to action to be taken by the Division in the event of Germans not signing Peace. The Division will move into Cologne and outskirts - The 3rd. Light Brigade East of the River. Training as usual. 3rd. Light Brigade No.G.S. 20/2.	App. No. 2.
	23-5-19.		Training and Education. G.O.C. and B.M. visited area to be occupied in the event of a move forward.	
	24-5-19.		3rd. Light Brigade Order No. 3 - referring to possible move forward to Cologne Area. Attached as Appendix No. 3. Empire Day - Holiday.	App. No. 3.

Army Form C. 2118.

WAR DIARY
or
INTELLIGENCE SUMMARY.
(Erase heading not required.)

Instructions regarding War Diaries and Intelligence Summaries are contained in F. S. Regs., Part II. and the Staff Manual respectively. Title pages will be prepared in manuscript.

- 3 -

Place	Date	Hour	Summary of Events and Information	Remarks and references to Appendices
BEDBURG	25-5-19.		Brigade Church Parade.	
	26-5-19.		Education and Training.	
	27-5-19.		Training as usual.	
	28-5-19.		Training as usual.	
	29-5-19.		51st. and 53rd. Bns. The Rifle Brigade inspected by the Commander-in-Chief, Rhine Army, at BEDBURG, at 0930 hours. Battalions were drawn up in Mass and received the C. in C. with a General Salute. The C. in C. inspected Companies, after which Battalions with transport marched past in column of route. The turn-out was good. 3rd. Light Brigade G.S. Nos. 11/11 and 11/11/2.	App. Nos 4 & 5.
	30-5-19.		The Divisional Commander inspected Cookhouses and Canteens etc. of 51st. and 53rd. Rifle Brigade, commencing at 1050 hours. Training and Education as usual.	
	31-5-19.		Divisional Commander inspected Cookhouses etc. of 52nd. Rifle Brigade at 1100 hours. Training and Education as usual.	

5/6/19

K.B. Seymour
Lieut-Colonel
Comdg 3rd Rifle Brigade

3RD. LIGHT BRIGADE ORDER NO. G.S.476.

WARNING ORDER.

4th. May 1919.

Copy 2a
APP N°1

1. H.R.H. THE DUKE OF CONNAUGHT will inspect the Brigade on Tuesday, 6th. instant.

2. The Brigade will be formed up on the parade ground by about 3.45p.m., and will receive H.R.H. The Duke with a general salute.
After the inspection, the Brigade will march past.
The Band of the 1st. Battalion, K.R.R.C., will be on parade.

3. The Brigade will form up in line of Battalions in quarter column with open ranks.
Order of Battalions from right to left will be:-
51st. Battalion The Rifle Brigade, 52nd. Battalion, 53rd. Battalion.

4. All officers will be dismounted.
No Transport to accompany Battalions.
Companies will be sized for ceremonial.
All other ranks will be in the ranks, except four sergeants per company (to include C.S.M. and C.Q.M.S., if on parade).

5. Battalions will be prepared to send adjutants and markers to meet the Brigade Major on the parade ground at about 3.30.p.m. Adjutants must know frontage required by their Battalions.

6. Lorries have been detailed to fetch the 52nd. Battn. The Rifle Brigade from KONIGSHOVEN to BEDBURG on the morning of the 6th. May. Cookers of this Battalion will be sent on in advance.
The Officer Commanding 51st. Battalion The Rifle Brigade will arrange suitable place for 52nd. Battalion to bivouac and have dinners.

7. Further details will be issued.

Captain,
/Brigade-Major, 3rd. Light Brigade.

DISTRIBUTION.

```
Copy No.  1. File.
 "    "   2. War Diary.
 "    "   3. G.O.C.
 "    "   4. Brigade Major.
 "    "   5. Staff Captain.
 "    "   6. Staff Captain (Civil Duties).
 "    "   7. Brigade Signal Officer.
 "    "   8. Brigade Intelligence Officer.
 "    "   9. 51st. Bn. The Rifle Brigade.
 "    "  10. 52nd. Bn. The Rifle Brigade.
 "    "  11. 53rd. Bn. The Rifle Brigade.
 "    "  12. 3rd. Light T.M. Battery.
 "    "  13. 157th. Field Company, R.E.
 "    "  14. 6th. Field Ambulance.
 "    "  15. No. 4 Company Train.
 "    "  16. Light Division "G".
 "    "  17. Light Division "Q".
```

For information only (handwritten, bracketing items 13–17)

3RD. LIGHT BRIGADE.

ORDER NO. 2.

B.A.O.R. Germany.   5th. May, 1919

1. HIS ROYAL HIGHNESS, Field Marshal, THE DUKE OF CONNAUGHT, will inspect the Brigade (less Transport and T.M.Battery) at 16.00 hours on TUESDAY, 6th. May.

2. PLACE OF PARADE.

Football field of the 51st Bn. The Rifle Brigade, at the junction of the BEDBURG - FRAUWEILER and BEDBURG - BUCHHOLZ Road.

2. DRESS.

(a) Drill Order with Steel Helmets.
Braces will NOT be worn by O.Ranks, and only one pouch will be worn, on the Right side.
Officers will wear "Sam Browne" Belts with one Brace and Revolver.

(b) No Sticks will be carried by any Officers.

(c) All Officers will be dismounted. No Horses on parade.

3. FORMATION.

(a) The Brigade will be formed up in line of Battalions in quarter Column.
Battalions will reach Parade Ground as follows:-

    51st. Bn. The Rifle Brigade.   15.30 hours.
    52nd. Bn. The Rifle Brigade.   15.35 hours.
    53rd. Bn. The Rifle Brigade.   15.40 hours.

(b) Officers will take Posts as in Review Order, sized by Battalions from the flanks to the Centre and dressed from the right of the Brigade.

(c) Companies will be equalised and sized, told off as for Ceremonial, and all Ranks will be dressed from the right of the Brigade. All O.Ranks will be in the ranks except four Sergeants per Company (to include C.S.M. and C.Q.M.S. if on parade).

(d) The Band of the 1st. K.R.R.C. will be formed up in rear of the centre of the Centre Battalion.

(e) Order of Battalions from right to left will be 51st. Bn. The Rifle Brigade, 52nd. Bn. The Rifle Brigade, 53rd. Bn. The Rifle Brigade.

5. ARRIVAL.

HIS ROYAL HIGHNESS will arrive by car, and will inspect the Brigade on Foot.

(2)

6. **SALUTE.**

As soon as HIS ROYAL HIGHNESS steps on to the Parade Field, the Union Jack will be broken, and a Royal Salute will be given.

The Band will play the first six lines of the "National Anthem", and all the Officers will salute with the hand.

The executive word of command for the Royal Salute will be given by the Brigadier who will be in front of the Centre of the Brigade.

7. **INSPECTION.**

Arms will be ordered on the executive word of Command of the Brigadier, and HIS ROYAL HIGHNESS will probably walk round the Ranks.

8. **MARCH PAST.**

On conclusion of the inspection the Brigade will march past HIS ROYAL HIGHNESS, in column of route.

Battalions will move off from the left, 53rd. Battalion The Rifle Brigade leading.

The Band will march in front of the leading Battalion as far as the saluting point, when it will wheel to the right, and form up and play all the Battalions by.

HIS ROYAL HIGHNESS will be on a raised platform, on the right of the road along which the Brigade marches, at the small open space near the Brigade Mess. The flag of the Rifle Brigade will fly at this point.

The Officers of each Company will march half in front and half in rear of the Company.

The executive word of Command for the Salute during the March past will be given by the Company Commander.

After passing the Saluting Point Battalions will move to their respective Parade Grounds, and break off.

Troops are not to halt in the main street after passing the Saluting point.

9. **MARKERS.**

Adjutants with markers and a guide to lead in the Battalions, and a N.C.O. from the Band of the 1st. K.R.R.C., will meet the Brigade Major on the Parade Ground at 15.15 hours.

R H Dowden
Captain,
Brigade Major, 3rd. Light Brigade.

DISTRIBUTION.

Copy No. 1. File.
        2. War Diary.
        3. G.O.C.
        4. Brigade Major.
        5. Staff Captain.
        6. Staff Captain, (Civil Duties).
        7. Brigade Signal Officer.
        8. Brigade Intelligence Officer.
        9. 51st Bn. The Rifle Brigade.
      10. 52nd Bn. The Rifle Brigade.
      11. 53rd Bn. The Rifle Brigade.
      12. 3rd Light T.M.Battery.)
      13. 157th Field Co. R.E.   )
      14. 6th Field Ambulance.   )   for information.
      15. No.4 Company Train.   )
      16. Light Division. "G".   )
      17. Light Division. "Q".   )
      18. Bandmaster. 1st K.R.R.C.

SECRET.

3rd LIGHT BRIGADE.
****

BEDBURG, Germany. 21st May, 1919.

1. In the event of the Germans not signing the peace treaty it will be necessary for the Brigade to move to the COLOGNE and take over guards and duties of the Division moving forward from that area.

2. The move to COLOGNE area will be by three stages of one day each. The earliest day for the Brigade to move will be the 25th inst.

3. Units will move complete

   DRESS :- Fighting Order.

   Lorries will be provided to carry men's packs.

4. Although full instructions for any move will be issued, Commanders must consider the possibility of a move and what will be required.

5. Acknowledge.

(sgd) C.H. DOWDEN, Captain,

Brigade Major, 3rd Light Brigade.

51st Bn. The Rifle Brigade.
52nd Bn. The Rifle Brigade.
53rd Bn. The Rifle Brigade.
157th Field Coy. R.E.
6th Field Ambulance.
No. 4 Coy. Train.
3rd Light T.M.B.

War Diary Op/ No 3   COPY No. 2

3RD. LIGHT BRIGADE.

SECRET.

ORDER NO. 3

24th. May 1919.

1. The Light Division is to be prepared to move to the COLOGNE area and relieve guards etc. at present furnished by the NORTHERN, LONDON, and LOWLAND Divisions.

2. The 3rd. Light Brigade will be prepared to move by march route to the area COLN DEUTZ, COLN KALK, and MULHEIM in accordance with movement table attached.

3. The dates in connection with moves will be known as follows:-
   First day on which any troops of the Division would move J-3 day
   Second day, J-2 day,
   Third day, J-1 day,
   Fourth day, J day,
   Fifth day, J ± 1 day, etc.

4. 51st. Bn. The Rifle Brigade will take over all guards now furnished by the 1st. London Brigade (List will be forwarded) before 1200 hours on J day.
   53rd. Bn. The Rifle Brigade will take over guards now furnished by 52nd. Royal Warwickshire Regiment on arrival at MULHEIM.

5. The P.R.O. and P.R.O's Police will remain in the present area at the disposal of the Civil Staff Captain.

6. Units will move complete with all their personnel and baggage as for a change of Station.
   Troops will march in "Fighting Order".
   Lorries, probably about 3 per battalion, will be available to assist in the moving of baggage and stores.
   All surplus stores which cannot be taken on the day of the move will be made into a dump at unit headquarters and left under a guard. All guards and dumps so left will be notified to Brigade Headquarters by wire.
   Bad marchers and weak men should be utilised for these guards.

7. Accommodation in the stageing areas is limited. Units will "close billet" or bivouac, whichsoever is most convenient to them.

8. Defence Schemes will be taken over from relieved units by all concerned.

9. 3rd. Light Brigade Headquarters will close at BEDBURG at 1000 hours on J ± 1 day, and open at HIELENFORST on arrival.

Acknowledge.

C.H. Dowden.
Captain,
Brigade Major,
3rd. Light Brigade.

DISTRIBUTION.

File.
War Diary.
G.O.C.
Brigade Major.
Staff Captain.
Staff Captain (Civil Duties).
Brigade Signal Officer.
Brigade Intelligence Officer.
51st. Bn. The Rifle Brigade.
52nd. Bn. The Rifle Brigade.
53rd. Bn. The Rifle Brigade.
3rd. Light T.M. Battery.
157th. Field Company, R.E.
6th. Field Ambulance.
No. 4 Company Train.
Light Division "G".
Light Division "Q".
P.R.O.
1st. London Brigade.

MOVEMENT TABLE ISSUED WITH 3rd LIGHT BRIGADE ORDER NO: 2. Dated 24th May, 1919.

Serial No.	Date	UNIT.	From.	To.	Route.	Remarks.
1	J-2	53rd Rifle Brigade	BEDBURG.	POULHEIM.	FRAUWEILLER - AUENHIEM - BUSDORF	
2	J-2	51st Rifle Brigade	BEDBURG.	GLESSEN - FLIESTEDEN.	BERGHEIM - BUSDORF.	
3	J-2	52nd Rifle Brigade	KONIGSHOVEN.	STOMMELN.	FRIEMERSDORF - ROMMERSKIRCHEN.	
4	J-2	157th Field Coy. R.E.	BUCHHOLZ.	BUSDORF.	FRAUWEILLER - HUCHELHOVEN.	
5	J-2	No. 4 Coy. Train.	BLERICHEM.	OBR: AUSSEM.	BERCHIEM.	
6	J-2	No. 6 Field Ambulance.	KASTER.	HUCHELHOVEN.	FRAUWEILER.	
7	J-2	T.M. Battery.	MILLENDORF.	BUSDORF.	FRAUWEILER.	
8	J-1	53rd Rifle Brigade.	POULHEIM.	Camp, BICKEN- DORF AREA.	DIRECT.	
9	J-1	51st Rifle Brigade.	GLESSEN.	CAMP, BICKEN- DORF AREA.	BRAUWEILER - BOCKLEHUND.	
10	J-1	52nd Rifle Brigade.	STOMMELN.	CAMP, BICKEN- DORF AREA.	DIRECT.	

Serial No.	Date.	UNIT.	From.	To.	Route.	Remarks.
11	J - 1	157th Field Coy. R.E.	BUSDORF.	CAMP, BICKENDORF AREA.	BRAUWEILER - BROCKLEMUND.	
12	J - 1	No. 4 Coy. Train.	OBR AUSSEM	CAMP, BICKENDORF AREA.	GLESSEN - DOCKLEMUND.	
13	J - 1	No. 6 Field Ambulance.	HUCKLEHOVEN.	CAMP, BICKENDORF AREA.	STOMMELN - DIRECT.	
14	J - 1	T.M. Battery.	BUSDORF.	CAMP, BICKENDORF AREA.	FRAUWEILER - BOCKLEMUND.	
15	J	53rd Rifle Brigade.	BICKENDORF.	MULHEIM.	Cross river by the MULHEIM BRIDGE.	H.Q. & 2 Coys.) Take 1 Coy. DELLBRUCK) over 1 Coy. LEVERKUS) from EN.)32nd Warwick Regt.
16	J	51st Rifle Brigade.	- do -	COLN KALK.	DIRECT.	To send an Offr. & O.R. by trams and take over all guards before 1200 hours on J day.
17	J	157th Field Coy. R.E.	- do -	NOTIFIED LATER.		
18	J	No. 4 Coy. Train.	- do -	COLN KALK.	DIRECT.	
19	J	No. 6 Field Ambulance.	- do -	MULHEIM.	To cross river by MULHEIM BRIDGE.	
20	J	T.M. Battery.	- do -	MULHEIM.	- do -	
21	J + 1	52nd Rifle Brigade.	- do -	COLN KALK.	DIRECT.	
22	J + 1	H.Q. 3rd Light Bde.	BEDBURG.	MIELENFORST.	DIRECT.	

* Time of Start will be notified to units daily.

War Diary

COPY NO.....2......

S E C R E T.

ADDENDUM NO. I to 3RD. LIGHT BRIGADE

ORDER NO. 3.

1. Light Division Administrative Instructions No. 107/12/33, dated 26/5/19, are forwarded for information and necessary action. (Issued to Units of Brigade Group only).

2. Reference Para. 5.c.

   TENTS.

   Units will report proposed location of dumps to Brigade Headquarters by 1200 hours, 28th. instant.

3. Reference Para. 6.

   BAGGAGE DUMPS.

   Units will report by wire to Brigade Headquarters, previous to moving, the number of lorries required to move furniture, etc.

4. Reference Para. 10.

   LORRIES.

   (a)   3 lorries per battalion, 1 each to 157 Field Coy., R.E. and No. 4 Company Train, will report at Headquarters of Units concerned on evening J – 3 day.
         These lorries will remain with Units until J day, and will be used for conveyance of baggage and advanced parties.

   (b)   2 additional lorries will report at Headquarters, 51st. Rifle Brigade, on J – 1 day to convey advanced parties for guards to COLN KALK.

ACKNOWLEDGE.

[signature]

Captain,
Brigade Major,
3rd. Light Brigade,

DISTRIBUTION:

To all recipients of 3rd.
Light Brigade Order No. 3.

War Diary

3rd LIGHT BRIGADE.

BEDBURG, Germany.   27th May, 1919.

1. The Commander-in-Chief will inspect the Brigade, including Transport, on the morning of the 29th inst.

2. **PLACE OF PARADE.**

   The Football Field of the 21st Bn. The Rifle Brigade, at the junction of the BEDBURG - FRAUWEILER and BEDBURG - BUCHOLZ Roads.

3. **DRESS.**

   Fighting Order as laid down in this office letters No.G.S.11/1 of 8.5.19 and G.S.11/1/1 of 15.5.19.
   Gloves will not be worn.

4. **FORMATION.**

   The Brigade will be formed up in Mass with transport in rear of units.
   The 16th K.R.R.C. band will be in rear of the centre of the transport.

5. **SALUTE.**

   On the arrival of the C. in C. the UNION JACK will be broken and a General Salute will be given.
   The executive word of command for the Salute will be given by the Brigadier.
   Officers will salute with the right hand.

6. **INSPECTION.**

   Arms will be ordered on the executive command of the Brigadier and the C.inC. will inspect the Brigade.

7. **MARCH PAST.**

   On the conclusion of the inspection the Brigade will march past in column of route.
   Battalions will move off from the left, the 23rd Bn. The Rifle Brigade leading.
   Transport will follow each battalion.
   The band will march in front of the leading battalion to the saluting point when it will wheel to the right and play the other battalions past.
   The saluting point will be the same as for the inspection by H.R.H. the Duke of Connaught.
   After passing the saluting point Battalions will move off to their respective parade grounds and disperse.
   Troops or transport will not halt in the main street after passing the saluting point.

8. **TIMES.**

   Time of parade of battalions and markers will be issued later.

9. **PARADE STATES.**

States will be compiled in accordance with this office letter No.G.S.11 of 6.5.19.

A copy of this state will be forwarded to Brigade Headquarters four hours before the time of parade.

The original will be brought on parade by the unit.

ACKNOWLEDGE.

C H Dowden

Captain,

Brigade Major, 3rd Light Brigade.

Distribution :- 51st Bn. The Rifle Brigade.
52nd Bn. The Rifle Brigade.
53rd Bn. The Rifle Brigade.
3rd Light T.M.B.
War Diary.
Light Division "G" (For information).

War Diary   A.D. No **5**

3rd LIGHT BRIGADE.

BEDBURG, Germany.   28th May, 1919.

INSTRUCTIONS FOR THE INSPECTION BY THE C. in C.

1. **TIME OF PARADE.**

   The Brigade will be formed up in lines of battalions in mass at 09.30 hours.
   Battalions will arrive on the parade ground complete with transport at the following times :-

        51st Rifle Brigade   08.30 hours
        53rd Rifle Brigade   08.45 hours

2. **MARKERS.**

   Adjutants with markers will meet the Brigade Major at the parade ground at 08.15 hours.

3. **TRANSPORT.**

   Every vehicle except baggage and supply wagons will be on parade.
   Transport will form up in one line behind the battalion in following order :- Cookers on the right, water carts, Lewis Gun limbers, ammunition limber tools, Medical cart, Mess cart and pack animals.

4. **PERSONNEL.**

   Every available man must be on parade, and only absolutely essential employed men left off parade.
   Parade states compiled in accordance with G.S.11 of 8th May 1919 will be forwarded to this office in duplicate by 15.30 hours on 26th inst. A copy of this state will be taken on parade by units.

5. **DRESS.**

   Dress for parade will be fighting order. Gloves will <u>not</u> be worn. Sticks will <u>not</u> be carried.
   All Officers, except the Transport Officer will be <u>dismounted</u>.

6. **DRESSING ON PARADE.**

   Special attention must be paid to dressing both on parade and during the march past.
   Troops will march in the centre of the road when marching past in column of route.
   All Officers and N.C.Os will march in the sections of fours.
   There will not be more than one incomplete section of fours in each platoon.

7. **SALUTING.**

   (a) On parade.
   The white signal flag will be worked from the window in front to assist the troops in moving together for the general salute in the same manner as for the last inspection.

2.

SALUTING (continued)

(b) During march past.

Officers will complete the salute and command "EYES RIGHT" on reaching the small flag which is 6 paces before arriving at the saluting point, and remain at the salute until 6 paces beyond. They will give the command "EYES FRONT" when the rear of their command has reached a point 6 paces beyond the saluting point.
The above points will be marked by flags.

8. OFFICERS.

If the C. in C. walks round the ranks he will be accompanied by the C.O. who will keep on his outer flank.
Company and Platoon Commanders will not fall out to accompany the Inspecting Officer unless ordered to do so.
On the march past Commanding Officers will remain in front of their battalions until they arrive at the Brigade Mess, when they will return and remain in rear of the Saluting Point.

9. INSTITUTES etc.

The C. in C. will most probably inspect a Cookhouse or Mess Room of the 51st Rifle Brigade in the SCHLOSS after the march past, and possibly the Officers Mess.

                         Captain,
           Brigade Major, 3rd Light Brigade.

Distribution :-   51st Bn. The Rifle Brigade.
                  53rd Bn. The Rifle Brigade.
                  War Diary.

Army Form C. 2118.

WAR DIARY
or
INTELLIGENCE SUMMARY.
(Erase heading not required.)

HEADQUARTERS, 3RD LIGHT BRIGADE.

Instructions regarding War Diaries and Intelligence Summaries are contained in F.S. Regs., Part II. and the Staff Manual respectively. Title pages will be prepared in manuscript.

Place	Date	Hour	Summary of Events and Information	Remarks and references to Appendices
BEDBURG.	1.6.19.		Brigade Church Parade.	
	2.6.19.		Training as usual. (Brigadier General went on leave).	
	3.6.19.		Birthday of H.M. The King. Brigade paraded at 10.00 hours and gave a Royal Salute and Cheers. Remainder of the day observed as a holiday. (3rd Light Brigade Order No.4).	APP. No.1
	4.6.19.		The usual Platoon Training and Musketry on the 30 yd. ranges carried out.	
	5.6.19.		The usual Training and Musketry.	
	6.6.19.		Platoon Training.	
	7.5.19.		- do -	
	8.6.19.		Brigade Church Parade at 10.00 hours in Y.M.C.A. - Sports of 51st Bn. The Rifle Brigade in afternoon.	
	9.6.19.		HOLIDAY. Major General Sir R.D. WHIGHAM, K.C.B., D.S.O. came to say Good Bye before proceeding to England to command the 3rd Division - Major General G.D. JEFFREYS C.B.,C.M.G. who is relieving him here came over with him. Sports of 52nd Bn. The Rifle Brigade at KONIGSHOVEN.	
	10.6.19.		Training and Education - Boxing Competition 53rd Bn. The Rifle Brigade.	
	11.6.19.		Training and Education - Boxing Competition 53rd Bn. The Rifle Brigade - Rifle Meeting 51st Bn. The Rifle Brigade.	
	12.6.19.		Usual Training.	
	13.6.19.		Training and Education. The Corps Commander went round Battalions in the afternoon, he inspected various cookhouses, institutions and messing arrangements and expressed satisfaction at what he saw.	
	14.6.19.		Training as usual.	

Army Form C. 2118.

WAR DIARY
or
INTELLIGENCE SUMMARY.
(Erase heading not required.)

Instructions regarding War Diaries and Intelligence Summaries are contained in F.S. Regs., Part II. and the Staff Manual respectively. Title pages will be prepared in manuscript.

Place	Date	Hour	Summary of Events and Information	Remarks and references to Appendices
BEDBURG.	15.6.19.		Brigade Church Parade - The Divisional Commander attended Church Parade - Battalions marched past after Church and then the Divisional Commander inspected the Camp of the 53rd Bn. The Rifle Brigade.	
	16.6.19.		Training - The Divisional Commander visited the 53rd Bn. The Rifle Brigade at Training.	
	17.6.19.		Orders received that J-3 day would be 17th June - Packing and getting ready for move. (3rd Light Brigade Order No.3).	APP.No.2
GILL.	18.6.19.		J-2 day. Brigade Group march moved forward in accordance with previous orders and were located as follows for the night :- Brigade H.Q. GILL, 53rd Rifle Brigade POULHEIM, 52nd Rifle Brigade STOMMELN, 51st Rifle Brigade GLESSEN and FLIESTADEN, 157th Field Coy. R.E. BUSDORF, 3rd Light T.M.B. BUSDORF, No. 4 Coy. Train ENGLEDORF, 6th Field Ambulance HUCKELHOVEN. Troops marched well, very hot day but very few fell out - Divisional Commander inspected 51st and 52nd Bns. The Rifle Brigade on the march.	
SULZ COLOGNE.	19.6.19.		J-1 day. Forward march continued and units located for the night as under :- Brigade H.W. SULZ. Outskirts of COLOGNE, 51st Rifle Brigade NIPPE, outskirts of COLOGNE, 53rd Rifle Brigade BICKENDORF, outskirts of COLOGNE, 52nd Rifle Brigade MUNGERSDORF, remainder of Brigade Group in BOCKLEMUND - very hot - troops march well. Orders received in the evening that J day was postponed indefinitely and that further moves etc. were consequently similarly postponed except that 53rd Rifle Brigade would move to MULHEIM and take over guards and duties there from 18th K.R.R.C. on the following day.	
	20.6.19.		53rd Bn. The Rifle Brigade marched to MULHEIM and took over guards and duties there from 18th K.R.R.C., remainder of Brigade Group stands fast. Information received that J day would now most probably be Tuesday 24/6/19. Orders received that 52nd Bn. The Rifle Brigade were to move to SULZ, outskirts of COLOGNE on the following day. Brigadier General returned from leave.	
	21.6.19.		52nd Bn. The Rifle Brigade moved to School in Berrenrather Strasse, SULZ, outskirts of COLOGNE. No other moves.	

Army Form C. 2118.

WAR DIARY
or
INTELLIGENCE SUMMARY.
(Erase heading not required.)

Instructions regarding War Diaries and Intelligence Summaries are contained in F. S. Regs., Part II. and the Staff Manual respectively. Title pages will be prepared in manuscript.

Place	Date	Hour	Summary of Events and Information	Remarks and references to Appendices
SULZ, COLOGNE.	22.6.19.		Sunday. Church Parades - Divisional and Brigade Commanders attended Church with 52nd Bn. the Rifle Brigade. Orders received for march in the event of the Division being ordered back to its old area.	APP.No.3.
	23.6.19		Some training carried out near billets - 3rd Light Brigade Order No.5 issued.	
	24.6.19.		Divisional and Brigade Commanders inspected the guards furnished by 53rd Bn. The Rifle Brigade at MULHEIM - LEVERKUSEN and DELLBRUCK. Usual Training.	
	25.6.19.		Training and Education - Corps Commander inspected Billets etc. of 51st and 52nd Bns. The Rifle Brigade.	
	26.6.19.		Orders received to send 157th Field Coy. R.E. to BEDBURG to assist in preparing Camp for 2 Companies - 51st Bn. The Rifle Brigade ordered to evacuate the SCHLOSS which is required for a C.C.S. Some Training carried out.	
	27.6.19.		157th Field Coy. R.E. moved to BUCHHOLZ by Lorry - Brigadier General visited Guards furnished by 53rd Bn. The Rifle Brigade - Training etc. as usual.	
	28.6.19.		Some training carried out. Peace signed.	
	29.6.19.		Church Parade - Orders received that march back would commence on 30-6-19	
	30.6.19.		March back to BEDBURG Area, in accordance with Brigade Order No.5 (attached as appendix No.3).	
	4.7.19.			

Brigadier General,
Commanding, 3rd Light Brigade.

SECRET.
Copy No. 2

3rd LIGHT BRIGADE.

ORDER No. 4.

31st May, 1919.

1. **BIRTHDAY.**

    Tuesday, June 3rd., being the birthday of His Majesty the King, will be celebrated as detailed below:-

2. **PARADE.**

    (a) 51st and 53rd Rifle Brigades will parade on the football ground of the 51st Bn. The Rifle Brigade, at 09.45 hours.

    (b) 52nd Rifle Brigade will be formed up in line on parade ground near their billets, by 10.00 hours, under the Commanding Officer.

3. **DRESS.**

    Drill Order with Caps.

4. **SALUTE.**

    At 10.00 hours the Officer Commanding the parade will order a Royal Salute.

5. **CHEERS.**

    After the Salute the Officer Commanding the parade will order caps to be taken off and three cheers for His Majesty the King to be given.

6. All guards will turn out at 10.00 hours and give a Royal Salute, bugles sounding the Salute.

7. **HOLIDAY.**

    The remainder of the day will be observed as a holiday.

8. **GENERAL.**

    It must be made clear in all unit orders that the above parade is to celebrate the birthday of His Majesty the King.

    Acknowledge.

                                              Captain,
                        Brigade Major, 3rd Light Brigade.

```
Copy No. 1 to File.              Copy No. 8 to Bde. Intelligence
         2    War Diary.                          Officer.
         3    G.O.C.                       9    51st Rifle Bde.
         4    Brigade Major.               10   52nd Rifle Bde.
         5    Staff Captain.               11   53rd Rifle Bde.
         6    Staff Captain                12   3rd Light T.M.B.
                (Civil Duties)             13   Light Division "G".
         7    Bde. Signal Officer.         14   Light Division "Q".
```

War Diary   S E C R E T.

Reference march table attached to 3rd Light Brigade Order No. 3.

Times of Start on J-2 day will be as follows :-

U N I T.	Starting Point.	Time.	Remarks.
53rd Rifle Brigade.	Camp BEDBURG.	05.30 hours.	
51st Rifle Brigade.	BEDBURG.	07.30 hours.	
52nd Rifle Brigade.	KONIGSHOVEN.	07.30 hours.	
T.M.B.	MILLENDORF.	07.40 hours.	
157th Field Coy. R.E.	BUCHOLZ.	07.50 hours.	
No. 4 Coy. Train.	BLATZHEIM.	08.10 hours.	
No. 8th Field Amb.	KASTER.	08.30 hours.	
Brigade H.Q.	BEDBURG.	10.30 hours.	

                                                 Captain,
                             Brigade Major, 3rd Light Brigade.

To all recipients of
    3rd Light Brigade Order No 3.

War Diary

SECRET.

AMENDMENT No.1 to 3rd LIGHT BRIGADE ORDER No.3 dated 24.5.19.

1. Cancel march table and substitute attached.

2. Cancel para. 9. Brigade Headquarters will move as in march table.

3. Add new paras.

9. All troops of the Brigade Group moving into or through COLOGNE previous to 18.00 hours on J day will come under tactical orders of G.O.C., Northern Division on reaching BICKENDORF.

All troops of the Brigade Group moving east of the Rhine, except the battalion moving to MULHEIM Area previous to 18.00 hours on J day will come under the tactical orders of G.O.C., London Division on crossing the Rhine.

The battalion moving to MULHEIM Area will come under the tactical orders of II Corps on crossing the Rhine.

All troops of the Brigade group revert to the tactical orders of the G.O.C. Light Division at 18.00 hours on J day.

10. All units on arriving in billets will report the location of their Headquarters.

Units taking over guards or duties will, as soon as the relief is complete, forward to Brigade Headquarters daily a detailed list of guards or other duty taken over.

11. 52nd Rifle Brigade will detail one company to report to the Provost Marshal, Rhine Army at the Prisoner of War Cage at the Field Punishment Compound, SCHNURRGASSE, COLOGNE on J day.

The Company will live at the Cage and be accommodated under arrangements made with the Provost Marshall.

Acknowledge.

CH Dowden
Captain,
Brigade Major, 3rd Light Brigade.

To all recipients of
    3rd Light Brigade Order No. 3.

MOVEMENT TABLE ISSUED WITH AMENDMENT NO 1. to 3RD LIGHT BRIGADE ORDER No.3. Dated 24th MAY 1919

Serial No.	Date.	UNIT.	From.	To.	Route	Remarks
1.	J – 2	Brigade H.Q.	BEDBURG.	GILL		
2.	J – 2	53rd. Rifle Brigade	BEDBURG.	POULHEIM	FRAUWEILER–AUEHEIM–BUSDORF.	
3.	J – 2	51st. Rifle Brigade	BEDBURG.	GLESSEN–FLIESTEDEN.	BERGHEIM–BUSDORF.	
4.	J – 2	52nd. Rifle Brigade	KONIGSHOVEN	STOMMELN	FRITZDORF–ROTTESKIRCHEN.	
5.	J – 2	157th.FIELD COY.R.E.	BUCHHOLZ	BUSDORF.	FRAUWEILER–HUCHELHOVEN.	
6.	J – 2	No 4. Cow Train.	BLERICHEN	INGENDORF. RIELDT.	FRAUWEILER.	
7.	J – 3	No 6 Field Ambulance.	KASTER	HUCHELHOVEN	FRAUWEILER.	
8.	J – 2	T.M.BATTERY.	HILLENDORF.	BUSDORF.	FRAUWEILER.	
9.	J – 1	Brigade H.Q.	GILL	KANAL STRASSE SULZ	DIRECT.	
10.	J – 1	53rd. Rifle Brigade	POULHEIM	SCHOOL SUBERRATHER BICKENDORF.	DIRECT.	
11.	J – 1	51st. Rifle Brigade	GLESSEN	PULS STN SCHOOL. EHRENFELD.	BRAUWEILER–BOCKLEMUND.	
12.	J – 1	52nd. Rifle Brigade	STOMMELN	FORT & VILLAGE MUNGERS DORF.	DIRECT.	

Serial No.	Date.	Unit.	From.	To.	Route.	Remarks.
13	J - 1	157th Field Coy. R.E.	BUSDORF.	BOCKLEMUND.	BRAUWEILER - BOCKLEMUND.	
14	J - 1	No.4 Coy.Train.	OBERAUSSEM.	- do -	GIESSEN - DOCKLEMUND.	
15	J - 1	6th. Fd. Amb.	HUCKLEHOVEN.	- do -	STOMMELN - DIECT.	
16	J - 1	T.M. Battery.	BUSDORF.	- do -	FRAUWEILER - BOCKLEMUND.	
17	J	53rd. R.B.	BICKENDORF.	MULHEIM.	Cross River by the MULHEIM BRIDGE.	H.Q. & 2 Coys.) Take 1 Coy.BILLSRUCK) over 1 Coy.LEVERKUS) from ON.) 16th K.R.R. Corps.
18	J	51st. R.B.	EHRENFELD.	COLN KALK.	DIRECT.	To send on 52th. & by trams and take over all guards before 12 hours on J day.
19	J	157 BD.Coy.R.E.	BOCKLEMUND	51 Christian Gan Str. BRAUNSFELD.	DIRECT.	
20	J	No. 4 Coy. Trn.	- do -	COLN KALK.	DIRECT.	
21	J	6th Fd. Ambce.	- do -	HOHENBURG.	DIRECT.	
22	J	T.M. Battery	- do -	MULHEIM.	To cross River by MULHEIM BDGE.	
23	J - 1	52nd. R.B.	MUNGERSDORF.	COLN KALK.	DIRECT.	
24	J - 1	H.Q.3rd.Lt.Bde.	SULZ.	MIELENFORST.	DIRECT.	

* Time of Start will be notified to Units daily.

War Diary

SECRET.   Copy No...2...
*****

ADDENDUM No.1 to 3rd LIGHT BRIGADE ORDER No.8.

CIVIL ADMINISTRATION.

  The G.O.C. 3rd Light Brigade will reassume the duties of Sub-Area Commandant of the BEDBURG AREA at 1800 hours on "A" day.

                   J.K. Newberry
                        Captain,
             Staff Captain, 3rd Light Brigade.

Issued to all recipients of
3rd Light Brigade Order No.8.

War Diary

S E C R E T.

AMENDMENT NO. 3 TO 3RD LIGHT BRIGADE ORDER NO.5 DATED 23.6.19.

Reference March Table.

Cancel Serial No. 6.

157th Field Company R.E. will march to BUCHHOLZ on 27th inst.

[signature]
Captain,
Brigade Major, 3rd Light Brigade.

26th June 1919.

To all recipients of

3rd Light Brigade Order No.5.

War Diary

SECRET.

AMENDMENT NO. 2 to 3RD. LIGHT BRIGADE ORDER NO. 5,
dated 23/6/19.

----

1. The following units will complete the march back on the 2nd. day:-

   3rd. Light Brigade Headquarters.
   157th. Field Company, R.E.
   6th. Field Ambulance.
   No. 4 Coy. Light Divl. Train.

   Serials No. 2, 6, 7 and 8 of March table will be amended accordingly.

2. Cancel Serials No. 10, 15, 16 and 17 of March Table.

L.H. Dowden
Captain,
Brigade Major, 3rd. Light Brigade.

26/6/19.

To all recipients of 3rd.
Light Brigade Order No. 5.

War Diary

SECRET.

AMENDMENT NO.1 TO 3RD LIGHT BRIGADE ORDER NO.5 dated 25.6.19.

Para. 5 for "morning of third day" read afternoon of 2nd day.

March Table, Serial No.19.

Add to remarks column "Lorries and Busses to cross the MULHEIM Bridge before 10.00 hours.

W. Dowden
Captain,

23.6.19.

Brigade Major, 3rd Light Brigade.

To all Recipients
of 3rd Light Brigade Order No.5.

War Diary

SECRET.   COPY No. 2.

3rd LIGHT BRIGADE.

ORDER No. 5.   23rd June, 1919.

1. In the event of the Division being ordered back to its normal Area, the 3rd Light Brigade Group will move in accordance with table attached.

2. The first day as shown on movement table will be notified to all concerned by the Code word "HOME" followed by the date.

3. The following distances will be maintained on the march :-

   Between Companies ... 100 yards.
   Units and its
      Transport ... 100 yards.
   Battalions ... 500 yards.
   Transport of Units
      when Brigaded ... 100 yards.

   In addition vehicles of all kinds must have gaps of 50 yards between each Section of 12 vehicles.

4. DRESS.   Battle Order.

   Lorries will be provided for packs.

5. Guards furnished by the 53rd Rifle Brigade are being taken over by a Battalion of the Southern Division on the morning of the third day.

6. Advance parties will be sent on by units on the day before units move.

   The advance party of the 53rd Rifle Brigade will proceed from MULHEIM to BEDBURG by 2 lorries on 2nd day.

7. ACKNOWLEDGE.

                                    [signature]
                                    Captain,
                                    Brigade Major, 3rd Light Brigade.

Distribution :-
   Copy No. 1   File.
           2   War Diary.
           3   G.O.C.
           4   Brigade Major.
           5   Staff Captain.
           6   Staff Captain (Civil Duties).
           7   Brigade Signal Officer.
           8   Brigade Intelligence Officer.
           9   51st Bn. The Rifle Brigade.
          10   52nd Bn. The Rifle Brigade.
          11   53rd Bn. The Rifle Brigade.
          12   3rd Light T.M.B.
          13   187 Field Coy. R.E.
          14   6th Field Ambulance.
          15   No. 4 Coy. Train.
          16   Light Division "G".
          17   Light Division "Q"
          18   P.R.O. NORTHERN DIVISION
          19   1st Light Brigade.

MOVEMENT TABLE ISSUED WITH 3RD LIGHT BRIGADE ORDER NO. 5 DATED 22nd June 1915.

Serial No.	Date.	UNIT.	From	To.	Starting Point.	Time.	Route.	Remarks.
1	1st Day	NO MOVEMENT OF UNITS OF 3RD LIGHT BRIGADE.						
2	2nd Day	Brigade H.Q.	SULZ	GILL	KANAL STRASSE			
3	"	52nd Rifle Bde.	SULZ	STOTTLEN	Cross roads Southern end of MÜNGERSDORF.	06.00 hrs	BOCKLEMUND-STOTTLEN-ROTTSKIRCHEN.	
4	"	51st Rifle Bde.	NITTEL	POLLHEIM	EIFEL	06.00 hrs	BOCKLEMUND.	
5	"	I.M.B.	BOCKLEMUND	BUSDORF	IDDELDORF	05.15 hrs	DIRECT.	
6	"	157 Field Coy. R.E.	-do-	GLESSEN	-do-	05.30 hrs	-do-	
7	"	5th Field Amb.	-do-	-do-	-do-	06.15 hrs	-do-	
8	"	No.4 Coy. Train	-do-	INGENDORF	BOCKLEMUND	06.00 hrs Via STOTTLEN.		
9	"	Transport, 53rd Rifle Bde.	MÜLHEIM	POLHEIM	POLHEIM	06.00 hrs	DIRECT.	All except absolutely necessary Vehicles to be sent. Remainder by Serial No.12
10	3rd Day	Brigade H.Q.	GILL	BEDBURG	GILL			
11	"	52nd Rifle Bde.	STOTTLEN	KÖNIGSHOVEN	STOTTLEN	05.30 hrs	ROTTGEN-ESCHWEILER-NEURATH.	

Serial No.	Date.	UNIT.	From.	To.	Starting Point.	Time.	Route.	Remarks.
	3rd Day	51st Rifle Bde.	POULHEIM	BEDBURG.	POULHEIM	05.00 hrs	ROMMERSKIRCHEN-FRAUWEILER.	Take up billets & Camps in BEDBURG as before
12	"	Transport, 53rd Rifle Bde.	POULHEIM	BEDBURG	POULHEIM	05.20 hrs	Follow 51st Rifle Bde.	
13	"	T.M.B.	BUSDORF	MILLENDORF	BUSDORF	05.30 hrs	BUSDORF-NDR.AUSSEM-FRAUWEILER-BEDBURG.	
14	"	157 Field Coy.R.E.	GLESSEN	BUCHHOLZ	GLESSEN	05.30 hrs	BUSDORF-HUCHELHOVEN-FRAUWEILER.	
15	"	6th Field Amb.	-do-	KASTER	-do-	05.45 hrs	- do -	
16	"	No.4 Coy. Train	INGENDORF	BLEHICHEN	INGENDORF	06.00 hrs	Via BERGHEIM.	
17	"	Remainder of Transport from 53rd Rifle Bde. at Mulheim.	MULHEIM	POULHEIM	MULHEIM	06.00 hrs	DIRECT	Accommodation in POULHEIM from 2nd Light Bde.
18	"	53rd Rifle Bde. (less Transport)	MULHEIM	CAMP, BEDBURG	MULHEIM		DIRECT	By Lorry. Lewis Guns with 6 drums per Gun, to be taken in Lorries with Troops.
19	4th Day	Transport Serial 18 above	POULHEIM	BEDBURG	POULHEIM	08.00 hrs	DIRECT.	

Army Form C. 2118.

WAR DIARY
or
INTELLIGENCE SUMMARY.

3rd LIGHT BRIGADE HEADQUARTERS.

(Erase heading not required.)

Instructions regarding War Diaries and Intelligence Summaries are contained in F. S. Regs., Part II. and the Staff Manual respectively. Title pages will be prepared in manuscript.

Place	Date	Hour	Summary of Events and Information	Remarks and references to Appendices
BEDBURG. (Germany)	1.7.19.		Three Battalions and 3rd Light T.M.B. completed the move back to the BEDBURG Area. 52nd Bn. The Rifle Brigade took over the new Brigade Rifle Range at MORKEN from C.R.E., Light Division. Range is allotted to Battalions on two days in each week.	
	2.7.19.		The usual Training and Education carried out.	
	3.7.19.		Training and Education. 52nd Bn. The Rifle Brigade commenced firing on the MORKEN RANGE.	
	4.7.19.		Training as usual.	
	5.7.19.		Orders received that the Light Division was moving to the forward area to relieve the LOWLAND Division - Lowland Division to withdraw to this area. 3rd Light Brigade will relieve 3rd Lowland Brigade in accordance with 3rd Light Brigade Order No.6 attached, on 7th inst.	APP. No.1
	6.7.19.		Brigade Church Parade. All moves postponed 24 hours except that personnel to relieve frontier posts.	
	7.7.19.		Advance parties proceed to new area and relieved the frontier posts.	
	8.7.19.		Brigade proceed by rail and march route to BENRATH Area in accordance with Brigade Order No.6. Two trains were allotted for troops and baggage, entraining at BEDBURG at 07.30 hours and 09.00 hours, both trains very late. Two trains allotted for transport entraining from HOREM (about 10 miles from billeting area).	
BENRATH. (Germany)	9.7.19.		Moves ordered in Brigade Order No.6 completed and troops now located as follows :- Brigade H.Q. BENRATH, 51st Bn. The Rifle Brigade, HILDEN, 52nd Bn. The Rifle Brigade HILDEN, 53rd Bn. The Rifle Brigade BENRATH, 3rd Light T.M.B. BENRATH, 157th Field Coy. R.E. BENRATH, No.4 Coy. Train HILDEN - No.6 Field Ambulance moved to OHLIGS and came under 2nd Light Brigade Group. Brigade Commander visited frontier posts.	
	10.7.19.		Training and Education.	
	11.7.19.		- do -	
	12.7.19.		- do -	

Army Form C. 2118.

WAR DIARY
or
INTELLIGENCE SUMMARY.
(Erase heading not required.)

Instructions regarding War Diaries and Intelligence Summaries are contained in F. S. Regs., Part II. and the Staff Manual respectively. Title pages will be prepared in manuscript.

Place	Date	Hour	Summary of Events and Information	Remarks and references to Appendices
BENRATH. (Germany)	13.7.19.		Church Parade – Blackade removed except for, Chemicals, Dyes, Gold and Silver, Bullion, Securities, Arms and Munitions of War. Conflict ensued between patrol of 52nd Bn. The Rifle Brigade on the frontier about REIZHOLZ Station. Party of civilians were attempting to raid a train on the frontier, when challenged by patrol ran away and fired on patrol who returned fire. A fire fight lasting for about 15 minutes resulted in one civilian killed, two wounded, and seven captured. A wagon containing about 300 Motor Tyres which had been taken from the train was also captured. We had no casualties. Raiders were a known notorious gang from DUSSELDORF. Conflict occurred about 21.00 hours.	APP. No.2
	14.7.19.		Victory March Paris. One officer and 12 O.R. from Infantry of Brigade attended. G.O.C., Staff Captain, One officer and two O.R. witnessed the march. Training as usual for men not on frontier guards.	
	15.7.19.		Training as usual. Two civilians crossed the frontier by way of the wire in vicinity of REIZHOLZ Post, they were fired on and one captured – later sentry was fired on from a house in the neutral zone. No casualties.	
	16.7.19.		Training as usual.	
	17.7.19.		Training and Education. 3rd Light Brigade DEFENCE INSTRUCTIONS, BENRATH AREA, issued.	
	18.7.19.		Training and Education.	
	19.7.19.		Holiday – Peace Celebrations in ENGLAND.	
	20.7.19.		Church Parade.	
	21.7.19.		Usual Training. Battalions commence the General Musketry Course. The Divisional Commander went round the Perimeter of the Brigade.	
	22.7.19.		Training and Education.	

Army Form C. 2118.

WAR DIARY
or
INTELLIGENCE SUMMARY.
(Erase heading not required.)

*Instructions regarding War Diaries and Intelligence Summaries are contained in F. S. Regs., Part II. and the Staff Manual respectively. Title pages will be prepared in manuscript.

Place	Date	Hour	Summary of Events and Information	Remarks and references to Appendices
BENRATH. (Germany)	23.7.19.		Holiday - Peace Celebrations.	
	24.7.19.		Training and Education.	
	25.7.19.		Training etc. as usual.	
	26.7.19.		Training and Education.	
	27.7.19.		Church Parade. 51st Bn. The Rifle Brigade commenced General Musketry Course.	
	28.7.19.		Training, Musketry etc. G.O.C. inspected billets and institutions.	
	29.7.19.		Training, Musketry etc.	
	30.7.19.		Training as usual.	
	31.7.19.		- do -	

Brigadier General,
Commanding, 3rd Light Brigade.

31st July, 1919.

War Diary

APP No 1

SECRET.
Copy No. 2

3rd LIGHT BRIGADE.

5th July, 1919.

ORDER No. 6

1. The Light Division is relieving the Lowland Division in the Area BENRATH-OHLIGS-SOLINGEN. On relief the Lowland Division is withdrawing to the present Light Divisional Area.

2. The 3rd Light Brigade will move by rail on the 7th inst. to the Area BENRATH-HILDEN and relieve the 3rd Lowland Brigade.
   On completion of move the 3rd Light Brigade will be located as in Appendix "A" attached.
   Civil Administrative Staff and Personnel will proceed with the Brigade.

3. Dress for the move will be Battle Order - Distances as laid down in para. 1 of "Notes on March Discipline" will be maintained by all Units or part of Unit on the March.

4. Units will take over and man the frontier posts as shown in Appendix "B" attached.
   The date of these reliefs will be notified later.

5. Advance parties to arrange accommodation and reconnoitre frontier posts etc. will proceed to the new area on the 3th inst as already ordered.
   Advance parties from the 3rd Lowland Brigade are arriving at units H.Qrs. on 6th inst to take over accommodation etc.

6. (a) All details of relief will be arranged between Commanders concerned.

   (b) Defence Schemes, Regulations and Orders as to frontier posts and Civil Administration etc., and details of training facilities will be taken over from relieved units.

   (c) 53rd Rifle Brigade will take over the Rifle Range at URDENBACK and furnish 1 N.C.O. and 3 men as permanent Range Wardens.

   (d) All information regarding the present area together with Defence instructions will be handed over to the incoming units.

7. All tents, Barrack and Camp Stores etc. which is not Unit Mobilization equipment will be handed over to relieving units and receipt obtained.

8. Certificates as to cleanliness of billets, camps etc. will be forwarded to Brigade H.Q. by 09.00 hours on 9th inst.

9. Train arrangements will be forwarded later.

10. ACKNOWLEDGE.

Dowden
Captain,
Brigade Major, 3rd Light Brigade.

(P.T.O.)

Distribution :-

Copy No.
1. File.
2. War Diary.
3. G.O.C.
4. Brigade Major.
5. Staff Captain.
6. Staff Captain, Civil Duties.
7. Bde. Signal Officer.
8. Bde. Intelligence Officer.
9. 51st Rifle Brigade.
10. 52nd Rifle Brigade.
11. 53rd Rifle Brigade.
12. 3rd Light T.M.B.
13. 157th Field Coy. R.E.
14. 6th Field Ambulance.
15. No.4 Coy. Train.
16. Light Division "G".
17. Light Division "Q".
18. P.R.O.
19.)
20.) 3rd Lowland Brigade.
21.)
22.)
23. A.D.M.S. Light Division.
24. Light Divisional Train.
25. 2nd Light Brigade.
26.)
27.) Spare.
28.)
29.)

APPENDIX "A"

Serial No.	UNIT.	From.	To.	Taking over Accommodation from.	Relieved in present Area by.	REMARKS.
1	H.Q. 3rd Light Bde.	BEDBURG.	BENRATH.	3rd Lowland Bde. H.Q. BANHOF HOTEL.	3rd Lowland Bde.	
2	51st Rifle Bde.	BEDBURG.	HILDEN.	1/4 R.S. Fusiliers.	1/4 R.S. Fusiliers.	
3	52nd Rifle Bde.	KONIGSHOVEN.	HILDEN.	1/8 Scottish Rifles.	1/9 Scottish Rifles.	
4	53rd Rifle Bde.	BEDBURG, CAMP.	BENRATH.	9th Scottish Rifles.	9th Scottish Rifles.	
5	3rd Light T.M.B.	MILLENDORF.	BENRATH.	3rd Lowland T.M.B.	3rd Lowland T.M.B.	
6	157th Field Coy. R.E.	BUCHHOLZ.	BENRATH.	63rd Field Coy. R.E.	63rd Field Coy. R.E.	
7	No.4 Coy. Div. Train.	BLERICHEN.	HILDEN.	No.4 Coy. Low. Div. Tn.	No.4 Coy. Low. Div. Tn.	Billets etc. from 1/4 R.S. Fus. in HILDEN
8	No.6 Field Ambulance.	KASTER.	HILDEN.	New AREA.		

APPENDIX "B".

NUMBER AND NAME OF POST.	APPROXIMATE LOCATION.	At present found by	To be taken over by	Strength of Post.	REMARKS.
No. 1 Post KELPERDICK.	1 Mile S. of TRILLS.	1/4 R.S. Fusiliers.	51st Rifle Bde.	1 PLATOON complete.	
No. 2 Post DICKHAUS.	½ Mile N.E. of ELB.	-do-	-do-	1 PLATOON complete.	
No. 3 Post REISHOLZ	REISHOLZ.	-do-	-do-	1 PLATOON complete.	
No. 4 Post DAMMSTWG.	1½ Miles S. of ELLER.	-do-	52nd Rifle Bde.	1 PLATOON complete.	
No. 5 Post FRIEDHOF.	½ Mile N. of HOLTHAUSEN.	-do-	-do-	1 PLATOON complete.	
No. 6 Post HOLTHAUSEN.	HOLTHAUSEN.	1/8 Scottish Rifles.	-do-	2 PLATOONS complete.	
No. 7 Post HIMMELGEIST.	HIMMELGEIST.	-do-	53rd Rifle Bde.	2 PLATOONS Complete.	
No. 8 Post PATROL FORKS.	1 Mile S.E. of HIMMELGEIST.	-do-	-do-	2 PLATOONS complete.	

War Diary

SECRET.   COPY NO. 2

                                                      7th. JULY 1919.

AMENDMENT NO. 1 TO 3RD. LIGHT BRIGADE ORDER NO. 6.

1.   Mounted personnel and transport of 157th. Field Company, R.E., No. 4 Company Divl. Train and No. 6 Field Ambulance, will proceed to the new area by march route, in accordance with Movement table attached.
        Dismounted personnel of these units will proceed by train as already detailed.

2.   ACKNOWLEDGE.

                                                    Captain,
                                                Brigade Major,
                                              3rd. Light Brigade.

To all recipients of
3rd. Light Brigade Order No.6.

MOVEMENT TABLE FOR MOUNTED PERSONNEL AND TRANSPORT.

Serial No.	DATE.	UNIT.	FROM.	TO.	ROUTE.	Starting Point.	Time.	REMARKS.
1.	8/7/19.	No. 4 Coy. Train.	BIERICHEN.	NIEVENHEIM.	ROMMERSKIRCHEN - GOHR.	BIERICHEN.	Hours 0430	
2.	-do-	157th Fd.Coy.R.E.	BUCHOLZ.	-do-	-do-	BUCHOLZ.	0400	
3.	-do-	6th. Fd. Amb.	KASTER.	-do-	-do-	KASTER.	0410	
4.	9/7/19.	No. 4 Coy. Train.	NIEVENHEIM.	HILDEN.	Via UEDESHEIM - HIMMELGEIST Ferry.	NIEVENHEIM.	Arrive at Ferry at 0905 hrs.	As vehicles cross Ferry they will move direct to Billeting Area.
5.	-do-	157th Fd.Coy.R.E.	-do-	BENRATH.	-do-	-do-	Arrive Ferry at 1130 hrs.	
6.	-do-	6th. Fd. Amb.	-do-	HILDEN.	-do-	-do-	Arrive Ferry at 1330 hrs.	

War Diary

3rd LIGHT BRIGADE.

HO
3d LIGHT Bde
No. 0215
Date 6th July 1919

BEDBURG, Germany.

1. Personnel as detailed in Appendix "B" to Brigade Order No.4. will proceed by lorry on the 7th inst., and relieve Frontier Posts and Guard on Petrol Parks.

2. Lorries have been asked for to report to units as below. If and when sanctioned this will be confirmed by wire.

UNIT.	TIME.	NUMBER OF LORRIES.	HEAD OF COLUMN.	FACING.
22nd. R. Bde.	1900 hours	8.	At KONIGSHOVEN. Southern entrance to KONIGSHOVEN, on KONIGSHOVEN-KASTEN Rd.	SOUTH.
21st. R. Bde.	1200	8.	At BEDBURG. Head at Junctn. FRAUWEILER-BEDBURG and BUCHOLZ-BEDBURG Road.	FRAU-WEILER.
23rd. R. Bde.	1800	8.	At BEDBURG. On BEDBURG-BETTWEIN Road, East of River, Head of Column where this road meets the BEDBURG-FRAUWEILER Road.	NORTH.

3. The Senior Officer proceeding from each Battalion will wire 3rd. Light Brigade direct when posts etc. have been relieved.

4. ACKNOWLEDGE.

W H Dowden
Captain,
Brigade Major,
3rd. Light Brigade.

21st. Bn. The Rifle Brigade.
22nd. Bn. The Rifle Brigade.
23rd. Bn. The Rifle Brigade.

War Diary APP.№2

3RD. LIGHT BRIGADE.

BENRATH, Germany.   17th. July 1919.

SECRET

HEADQUARTERS,
3rd
LIGHT BRIGADE.
No. G.16/24
Date.........

DEFENCE INSTRUCTIONS.

1. ROLE.

    The role of the Brigade is to guard and control that portion of the perimeter of the Cologne Bridgehead allotted to the Brigade, and to maintain law and order and enforce the regulations laid down for the Occupied Territory.

2. PERIMETER.

    The perimeter of the Brigade Area will be guarded and controlled by means of Posts established on the channels of communication (road, rail and tram), which pass across the frontier and by patrolling the interval between posts by day and night.

    Each of these posts will consist of complete units, i.e. one or two platoons or companies, and will be commanded by an officer.

    Where necessary, smaller posts under N.C.Os. will be detached from the main post to control subsidiary roads etc.

    The headquarters of the unit which comprises the Post will be located at the Post.

    At each post a flag will be flown, (Union Jacks are being provided), and the guards will be mounted with all due ceremony. At all posts and guards, sentries will pay compliments and guards turn out as under the normal regulations for guards.

    Each Main or Subsidiary Post will always have two men on duty:-

(a) DURING HOURS OF DAYLIGHT.

    One sentry and one examiner, the sentry will be armed as such, and will NOT examine passes or individuals. The examiner will have his rifle in the sentry box for emergency, and will examine all passes and individuals, etc.

(b) DURING HOURS OF DARKNESS.

    Two sentries, both armed with rifles and fixed swords; One of these sentries only will act as examiner.

    Posts will be furnished as under:-

(P.T.O.)

No. of Post.	Name.	Location.	Strength.	By whom Furnished.	Remarks
1.	KEMPERDICK.	On the TRILLS-HILDEN Road, abt. 1 mile South of TRILLS.	1 Platoon	51st. R.B.	
2.	DICKHAUS.	½ mile S.E. of UNTERBACH.	1 platoon	51st R.B.	
3.	REISHOLZ.	REIZ, 1 mile S. of ELLER.	2 platoons	51st. R.B.	
4.	DAMMSTEG.	1 mile S. of ELLER.	2 platoons	52nd R.B.	
5.	FRIEDHOF.	½ mile N. of HOLTHAUSEN.	1 platoon.	52nd R.B.	
6.	HOLTHAUSEN.	HOLTHAUSEN.	1 company.	52nd R.B.	
7.	HIMMELGEIST.	HIMMELGEIST.	1 company.	53rd R.B.	

Railway Controls are furnished as under:-

Control.	Location.	By whom furnished.	Remarks.
HILDEN.	HILDEN RLY. STATION.	Permanent.	Under 51st. Rifle Bde.
REISHOLZ.	REISHOLZ RLY. STATION.	Permanent Post. Reinforced by 52nd. R.B.	Under 52nd. Rifle Bde.

PERMANENT GUARDS.

No.	Name.	Location.	Strength.	By whom furnished.	Remarks.
8.	Petrol Supply Depot.	On River 1 mile W. of BENRATH.	1 Coy.	53rd. R.B.	

Attention is directed to Appendix "A".

- 3 -

3. ORDERS FOR POSTS & SENTRIES.

Each guard will be provided with clear definite orders in writing, laying down its purpose and duties.

Each Sentry Post will likewise have orders in writing, laying down the duties of the sentry and the examiner. Copies of all the various passes, posted neatly on a separate board, will be kept in the examiner's sentry box.

These orders etc. must be kept up to date by units furnishing the posts.

4. INLYING PICQUETS.

In each unit 25% of the ration strength (after deducting number employed on posts and guards detailed in para. 2 of these Instructions), will be detailed daily as inlying picquet.

Inlying picquets will not remain under arms, and may take part in training, games and recreation etc. in the vicinity of billets. They must be capable of turning out at very short notice, in case of emergency.

5. ALARM SIGNAL.

(i) The Alarm Signal will be:-

    (a) The sounding of Strombus Horns, or

    (b) 3 peals on Church Bells.

(ii) The following are authorised to sound the Alarm:-

    (a) BENRATH - The Brigade Commander.

    (b) HILDEN - The Senior Battalion Commander.

(iii) If the Alarm is sounded in one sub-area, it will be taken up in others.

6. ACTION ON ALARM.

(a) Inlying picquets fall in.

(b) All troops will be recalled to billets and units will be ready to move at half-an-hour's notice.

(c) All single sentries will be doubled:-

(d) The following Guards will be mounted:-

    <u>51st. Bn. The Rifle Brigade.</u>

1 Section on HILDEN TELEPHONE EXCHANGE.

    <u>53rd. Bn. The Rifle Brigade.</u>

1 Section on BRIGADE HEADQUARTERS & SIGNAL OFFICE.

1 Section on BENRATH TELEPHONE EXCHANGE.

(P.T.O.)

6. (e) A proportion of hand grenades will be fused ready for use.

    (f) Transport will be harnessed, but not inspanned.

7. PRECAUTIONARY ARRANGEMENTS.

In the event of information of impending civil disturbances being received, the message "Precautionary Arrangements" will be sent out from these Headquarters.

The action to be taken will be as laid down in para. 6 of these Instructions.

8. ALARM POSTS.

All Units will have definite Alarm Posts, which must be known by all ranks.

The locations of these posts will be notified to these Headquarters as early as possible.

9. ACTION IN CASE OF CIVIL DISTURBANCES.

    (a) The main centres of probable civil disturbances so far as the Brigade Area are:-

        (i) <u>Inside the Brigade Area.</u>

        The OHLIGS-HILDEN-BENRATH Line.

        (ii) <u>Outside the Brigade Area.</u>

        The Town of DUSSELDORF.

    (b) Action will be taken as indicated in para. 6 of these Instructions.

    (c) Units concerned will occupy tactical localities, with a view to:-

        (i) Keeping HILDEN, BENRATH and HIMMELGEIST under control.

        (ii) Preventing the incursion of an armed mob from DUSSELDORF.

(Detailed instructions will be issued as Appendix "B" to these Instructions).

10. LOCAL PROTECTION.

Every Unit must have a scheme in writing for its own local protection in the event of civil disturbances. This will include the protection of its Headquarters, Signal Office, transport lines etc.

- 5 -

11. TESTS.

All units will hold frequent tests of falling in on their alarm posts, and occupying tactical points selected for occupation in case of emergency.

12. In the event of civil disturbances, cables will probably be cut. The Brigade Signals Officer, in conjunction with Units, will draw up and submit to these Headquarters schemes for as many alternative methods of communication as possible forward of Brigade Headquarters.

13. Defence Instructions of Units, and a copy of orders for posts, guard, controls and sentries, mentioned in para. 2, will be forwarded to these Headquarters within 7 days of the date of these Instructions.

14. ACKNOWLEDGE.

W.H. Dowden
Captain,
Brigade Major,
3rd. Light Brigade.

COPIES NO:-

1. File.
2. War Diary.
3. G.O.C.
4. B.M.
5. S.C.
6. S.C.C.D.
7. Bde. Sigs. Off.
8. 51st. Rifle Brigade.
9. 52nd. Rifle Brigade.
10. 53rd. Rifle Brigade.
11. 3rd. Light T.M.B.
12. 157th. Field Coy., R.E.
13. No. 4 Company Train.
14. Off. i/c Stn. Control, HILDEN.
15. " " " " REISHOLZ.
16. Light Division.
17.)
18.)
19.) Spare.
20.)
21.)
22.)

APPENDIX "A".

NEUTRAL ZONE.

O.I. 98 - PART III.

1. **OBJECT.**

    The Neutral Zone is a belt of country, averaging 10 kilometres in width, which divides occupied from unoccupied Germany, and over which the Allied Armies exercise control. The aim of this control is to ascertain that no measure is being taken in this zone with a view to military preparations of either an offensive or a defensive nature.

    The zone opposite the Cologne Bridgehead is called Neutral Zone, Sector II.

2. **CONTROL.**

    The control of Neutral Zone, Sector II, is exercised by G.H.Q. Intelligence (Neutral Zone Inspection Staff).

3. **GERMAN FORCES.**

    (a) The Neutral Zone Commander, H.Q., WIPPERFURTH, is responsible for the maintenance of order, and has the following troops (Police Forces) at his disposal:-

        1 Squadron Cavalry, located at LITORF.
        1 Squadron Cavalry, located at WIPPERFURTH.
        1 Battn. Infantry, located at REMSCHEID.
        Local Police and Gendarmerie.

    (b) German troops will wear yellow brassards, and the local police and gendarmerie white brassards.

    (c) German troops are only allowed within 2 kilometres of the western boundary of the Neutral Zone with the previous consent of the British Authorities. This does not apply to REMSCHEID, which place they are permitted to enter, if required to assist in keeping order. Local Police and Gendarmerie are allowed to be armed and to be within 2 kilometres of the western boundary of the Neutral Zone in the execution of their duty.

4. **BRITISH FRONTIER CONTROL.**

    (a) All persons attempting to cross the boundary between occupied territory and the Neutral Zone, except by the authorised control posts, will be fired upon, whether in occupied territory or not. If individuals are thereby killed or wounded in the Neutral Zone, the British authorities have the right to enter the Neutral Zone and bring them into occupied territory.

(P.T.O.)

4. (b) With the exception noted in sub-para. (a), British troops are forbidden the cross the boundary line into the Neutral Zone without reference to the General Staff at G.H.Q.

(c) To meet the case of firing taking place in the direction of our outpost line, or of the safety of our troops being endangered by any action, civil or military, on the part of the Germans, authority to order troops to enter the Neutral Zone is delegated to Corps Commanders, who, at their discretion, may further delegate this authority to subordinate commanders not below the rank of Brigade Commanders. Except in cases of great emergency, reference should, however, first be made to G.H.Q.

5. RIOTS AND DISTURBANCES.

British troops are not concerned with riots, strikes, or other disturbances that may take place in the Neutral Zone, except in so far as they affect the safety of our troops. Any information which may be obtained as to occurrences of this nature should, however, be forwarded at once to higher authority.

6. BRITISH CONTROL IN THE NEUTRAL ZONE.

The following are forbidden in the Neutral Zone:-

(a) The importation of, or formation of depots of arms, ammunition, or any war material, beyond what is absolutely necessary for the German police forces. Arms and ammunition belonging to civilians will be given up and stored by the civil authorities.

(b) Any work by military or civilian labour which might be considered as carrying out offensive or defensive operations. This includes the taking up or laying of railways, or changing in any way the present system.

(c) All visual signalling by military or civilians.

(d) All wireless stations.

(e) Aircraft flying over Neutral Zone.

(f) All camouflage work.

(g) The pursuit of game.

(h) The assembling of troops of neighbouring garrisons, or any military exercise except close order drill and short range (30 yds.) shooting.

(See para. 12 of this Appendix).

7. INFRINGEMENT OF REGULATIONS.

Any attempt on the part of the Germans to contravene the regulations is to be at once reported to G.H.Q.

- 3 -

8. PASSES.

Passes for Officers and other ranks to enter the Neutral Zone are only issued in special cases, on application to G.H.Q., Intelligence. Permanent passes are only issued to Corps Commanders and B.Gs. G.S. of Corps occupying sectors of the Cologne Bridgehead, certain members of the Cologne Sub-Commission of the Inter-Allied Railway Commission, A.D. Roads, G.H.Q., and the Neutral Zone Inspection Staff.

9. VISITS.

The Neutral Zone Inspection Staff is available to conduct officers into the Neutral Zone as shown below on application in advance by Corps, giving the time and place at which the Officer of the Neutral Zone Inspection Staff is to report:-

II Corps - Tuesdays in each week. VI Corps - Thursdays in each week.

X Corps - Saturdays in each week.

10. WHITE FLAG.

All Officers visiting the Neutral Zone will have a white flag displayed on their motor car, or, if riding, carried by an orderly.

N.B. - This Section embodies and supersedes the instructions contained in:-

  Second Army G.945, dated January 3rd.
  G.H.Q.G.T.76/17. " April 12th.
  " G.O.4/A. " " 25th.
  " I.a. 67. " " 16th.
  G.R.O. 2745. " May 10th.

12. RAISING OF BLOCKADE.

The blockade of Germany is raised as from 12th. July 1919 inclusive, with the following exceptions:-

(a) Export and Import of Arms and Munitions of War is forbidden.

(b) Export of dyes and chemical products, platinum, gold and silver, coin bullion and foreign securities, is forbidden without a licence.

(c) Movement of Coal and Coke remains subject to present regulations.

(d) Circulation of civilians between the ALLIED and NEUTRAL Area without a pass is forbidden.

War Diary

S E C R E T.

> HEADQUARTERS,
> 3RD
> LIGHT BRIGADE.
> No. GS/16/24/1
> Date.............

3rd LIGHT BRIGADE.
****

BENRATH, Germany.   24th July, 1919.

1.   Herewith Appendix "C" to 3rd Light Brigade Defence Instructions dated 17.7.19.

2.   ACKNOWLEDGE.

                                                            Dowden

                                                                 Captain,

                  Brigade Major, 3rd Light Brigade.

To all recipients of

    3rd Light Brigade Defence Instructions.

3RD. LIGHT BRIGADE.

BENRATH, Germany.   24th. July 1919.

APPENDIX "C".

DEFENCE INSTRUCTIONS.

SIGNAL SERVICES.

1. In the event of civil disturbances resulting in the cutting of telephone cables, the following system of communication will be adopted immediately.

   (A) **TELEPHONE.**

2. The lines between Brigade Signal Office and HOLTHAUSEN Barrier is buried as far as 116 Dusseldorf Strasse, HOLTHAUSEN.

   In the event of the overhead portion of the line being cut, the telephone at the Barrier will be disconnected from the Line and taken to the Test Box in the top floor of No. 116 Dusseldorf Strasse, and connected direct to buried portion of the line. The line is labelled in Test Box "3RD. LIGHT BRIGADE - HOLTHAUSEN".

   A Runner Service will then be organised between Telephone and Barrier.

3. The Line between Brigade Signal Office and FRIEDHOF Post is also buried to this Test Box, and similar action will be taken at this Post.

4. The Line to REISHOLZ STATION and Post is buried as far as Test Box in the top floor of "ZILS RESTAURANT" opposite the Station.

   Telephone in Station Control Post will be moved to this Test Box and connected to the line which is labelled "3RD. LIGHT BRIGADE to REISHOLZ POST".

5. The Signalling Officer, 52nd. Bn. The Rifle Brigade, will be responsible for supplying signallers to move the telephones.

   They must be familiar with positions of Test Boxes and the lines therein.

   (B) **VISUAL.**

6. Communication will be established as shown in Table below, immediately alarm is given.

   Battalion Signalling Officers concerned will be responsible for supplying signallers, lamps, etc.

   Communications by Visual will be practiced between these Points, at frequent intervals.

(P.T.O.)

FROM.	TO.	STATIONS MANNED BY.
BENRATH CHURCH TOWER.	REAL SCHULE, HILDEN.	Brigade Signals and 51st. R.B. respectively. (To serve 51st. & 52nd. Rifle Brigade).
BDE. CENTRAL STATION.	REISHOLZ POST.	Brigade Signals and 51st. Rifle Brigade respectively.
- do -	REISHOLZ STN.	Bde. Signals and 52nd. Rifle Brigade respectively.
REAL SCHULE, HILDEN.	DICKHAUS POST.	51st. Bn. Rifle Brigade.
HIMMELGEIST Post.	HOLTHAUSEN Barrier.	53rd. and 52nd. Rifle Brigade respectively.

(C) **WIRELESS.**

7. Wireless Loop Sets will be worked between REAL SCHULE, HILDEN, and KEMPERDICK Post.
   Personnel to be supplied by 51st. Bn. The Rifle Brigade.
   Loop Sets will be supplied by Brigade Signal Officer.

8. Attached Diagram shows complete communications.

To all recipients of 3rd. Light
Brigade Defence Instructions.

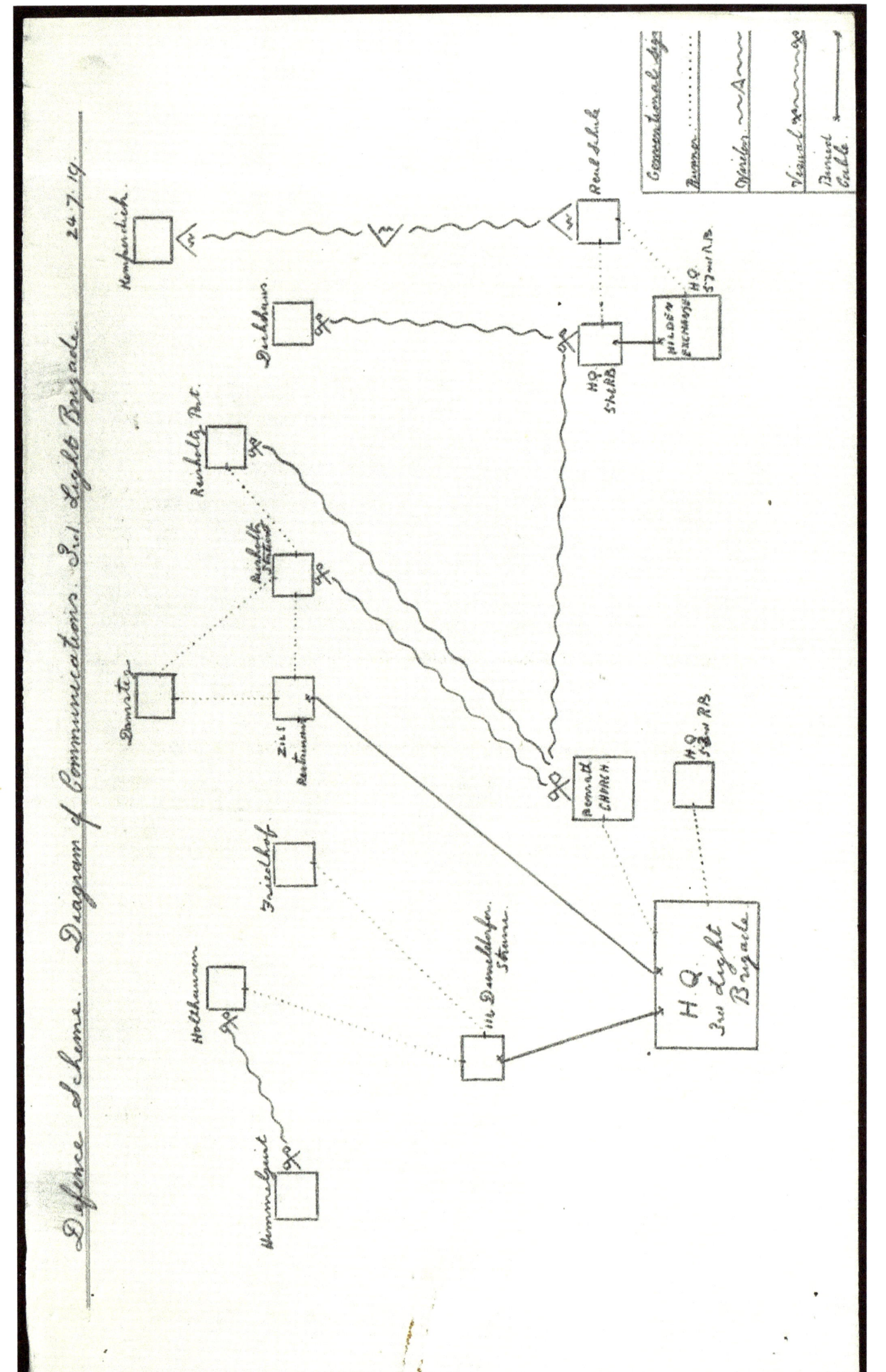

3rd LIGHT BRIGADE.
****

BENRATH, Germany.   3rd September, 1919.

      Herewith War Diary (in duplicate) of 3rd Light Brigade Headquarters for the month of August.

      Please acknowledge receipt.

                                                  Brigadier General,
                                Commanding, 3rd Light Brigade.

The Secretary,
   War Office,
      LONDON S.W.1.

Army Form C. 2118.

WAR DIARY
or
INTELLIGENCE SUMMARY.

HEADQUARTERS,
3RD LIGHT BRIGADE.
BENRATH., Germany.

(Erase heading not required.)

MONTH OF AUGUST.
****

Instructions regarding War Diaries and Intelligence Summaries are contained in F. S. Regs., Part II. and the Staff Manual respectively. Title pages will be prepared in manuscript.

Place	Date	Hour	Summary of Events and Information	Remarks and references to Appendices
BENRATH.	1/8/19.		Troops not employed on Perimeter Guard at Training, Education and Musketry. Remainder of 51st Bn The Rifle Brigade carrying out General Musketry Course. Troops on Perimeter line put out wire where not yet completed.	
do.	2/8/19.		Troops not employed on Perimeter Guard at Training, Education and Musketry - Remainder of 51st Bn The Rifle Brigade carrying out General Musketry Course - Troops on Perimeter line put out wire where not yet completed.	
do.	3/8/19.		Church Parade 2 Companies 51st Bn The Rifle Brigade firing General Musketry Course. House in HOLTHAUSEN suspected of containing arms raided - no arms found.	
do.	4/8/19.		Holiday - Training suspended.	
do.	5/8/19.		Training, Musketry and Education.	
do.	6/8/19.		Training, Musketry and Education.	

Sheet 1.

Army Form C. 2118.

WAR DIARY
or
INTELLIGENCE SUMMARY.
(Erase heading not required.)

Instructions regarding War Diaries and Intelligence Summaries are contained in F. S. Regs., Part II. and the Staff Manual respectively. Title pages will be prepared in manuscript.

Place	Date	Hour	Summary of Events and Information	Remarks and references to Appendices
BENRATH.	7/8/19.		Training, Musketry and Education.	
do.	8/8/19.		Usual Training and Education - Examination for Second Class Certificates of Education carried out in every Unit.	
do.	9/8/19.		Usual Training - Examination for Third Class Certificates of Education.	
do.	10/8/19.		Church Parade.	
do.	11/8/19.		51st. Bn The Rifle Brigade completed General Musketry Course - Other Units Training as usual.	
do.	12/8/19.		The Perimeter in front of RHISHOLZ STATION was advanced about 200 yards to prevent smuggling from the station. Training as usual.	
do.	13/8/19.		Training, Musketry and Education as usual.	

Sheet 2.

Army Form C. 2118.

WAR DIARY
or
INTELLIGENCE SUMMARY.
(Erase heading not required.)

Instructions regarding War Diaries and Intelligence Summaries are contained in F. S. Regs., Part II. and the Staff Manual respectively. Title pages will be prepared in manuscript.

Place	Date	Hour	Summary of Events and Information	Remarks and references to Appendices
BENRATH.	14/8/19.		Training, Musketry and Education as usual. G.O.C. inspected Billets etc, of 51st Bn The Rifle Brigade.	
do.	15/8/19.		Training, Musketry and Education as usual.	
do.	16/8/19.		Training, Musketry and Education as usual.	
do.	17/8/19.		Church Parades.	
do.	18/8/19.		Training and Education.	
do.	19/8/19.		Training and Education.	
do.	20/8/19.		Training and Education.	

Sheet 5.

Army Form C. 2118.

WAR DIARY
or
INTELLIGENCE SUMMARY.
(Erase heading not required.)

Instructions regarding War Diaries and Intelligence Summaries are contained in F. S. Regs., Part II. and the Staff Manual respectively. Title pages will be prepared in manuscript.

Place	Date	Hour	Summary of Events and Information	Remarks and references to Appendices
BENRATH.	21/8/19.		Brigade Sports. (Athletic Sports. 52nd Bn The Rifle Brigade. / Cross Country. 52nd Bn The Rifle Brigade. / Basket Ball. 3rd Light Bde. Headquarters. / Tug-of-War (Catch) Light Division, Headquarters. / Tug-of-War (Light) 51st Bn The Rifle Brigade. / Boxing. 2nd Bn. M.G.Corps.) 1 Cup winners	
do.	22/8/19.		Brigade Sports.	
do.	23/8/19.		Usual Training.	
do.	24/8/19.		Church Parades.	
do.	25/8/19.		Holiday - Birthday Sports - 3 Bns the Rifle Brigade.	
do.	26/8/19.		Training and Education as usual.	
do.	27/8/19.		Training and Education. All leave stopped owing to Division expecting to proceed home in about 3 weeks time.	

Sheet 4.

Army Form C. 2118.

WAR DIARY
or
INTELLIGENCE SUMMARY.
(*Erase heading not required.*)

Instructions regarding War Diaries and Intelligence Summaries are contained in F. S. Regs., Part II. and the Staff Manual respectively. Title pages will be prepared in manuscript.

Place	Date	Hour	Summary of Events and Information	Remarks and references to Appendices
BENRATH.	28/8/19.		Training and Education.	
do.	29/8/19.		Training and Education.	
do.	30/8/19.		Training and Education.	
do.	31/8/19.		Church Parades - 53rd Bn The Rifle Brigade Musketry.	

[signature] Brigadier-General,
Commanding., 3rd Light Brigade.

Headquarters,
3rd Light Brigade,
31st August 1919.

Sheet 5.

3rd LIGHT BRIGADE.

BENRATH, Germany.

30th September, 1919.

H. Q. 3rd LIGHT Bde
No. GS.5/69
Date ....

Herewith War Diary (in duplicate) of these Headquarters for the Month of September.

Please acknowledge.

Brigadier General,
Commanding, 3rd Light Brigade.

The Secretary,
   War Office,
      LONDON, S.W.1.

Army Form C. 2118.

WAR DIARY
or
INTELLIGENCE SUMMARY

(*Erase heading not required.*)

HEADQUARTERS,
3rd LIGHT BRIGADE.

Instructions regarding War Diaries and Intelligence Summaries are contained in F. S. Regs., Part II. and the Staff Manual respectively. Title Pages will be prepared in manuscript.

Place	Date	Hour	Summary of Events and Information	Remarks and references to Appendices
BENRATH, Germany.	1/9/19		Each Battalion has two Companies on duty on Perimeter Control Posts - 51st & 52nd Bn Rif. Bde have two Companies on Training and Education. 53rd Bn Rif. Bde has two Companies firing the General Musketry Course.	
	2/9/19		Training and Education.	
	3/9/19		Training and Education.	
	4/9/19		Divisional Sports.	
	5/9/19		Training and Education - Divisional Cross Country Run and Basket Ball Final.	
	6/9/19		Training and Education.	
	7/9/19		Church Parade.	
	8/9/19		Inspection of 51st & 52nd Bns. The Rifle Brigade by the Divisional Commander - After Inspection on Parade the G.O.C., saw one Company from each Battalion, at drill and one Company from each Battalion at manoeuvre - Result satisfactory.	
	9/9/19		The usual Training and Education.	
	10/9/19		The usual Training and Education.	
	11/9/19		The usual Training and Education.	

Sheet 1.

Army Form C. 2118.

WAR DIARY
or
INTELLIGENCE SUMMARY

(Erase heading not required.)

Instructions regarding War Diaries and Intelligence Summaries are contained in F. S. Regs., Part II. and the Staff Manual respectively. Title Pages will be prepared in manuscript.

Place	Date	Hour	Summary of Events and Information	Remarks and references to Appendices
BENRATH, Germany.	12/9/19.		The G.O.C. in Chief visited the area and interviewed Commanding Officers. Training as usual. Orders received that in the event of the Germans not fulfilling certain conditions a mixed force would march and occupy ELBERFELD - Similar forces from all the Allies would also advance and occupy selected towns.	
	13/9/19.		Training as usual.	
	14/9/19.		Church Parade.	
	15/9/19.		Training as usual.	
	16/9/19.		51st Bn The Rifle Brigade commence firing Lewis Gun Course and Casuals for General Musketry Course. Other Units Training as usual.	
	17/9/19.		The Corps Commander visited the area and saw certain of the Control Posts. Training and Education as usual.	
	18/9/19.		Training and Education as usual.	
	19/9/19.		Training and Education.	
	20/9/19.		Training and Education.	
	21/9/19.		Church Parade.	

Sheet 2.

Army Form C. 2118.

WAR DIARY
or
INTELLIGENCE SUMMARY

(Erase heading not required.)

Instructions regarding War Diaries and Intelligence Summaries are contained in F. S. Regs., Part II. and the Staff Manual respectively. Title Pages will be prepared in manuscript.

Place	Date	Hour	Summary of Events and Information	Remarks and references to Appendices
BENRATH, Germany.	22/9/19.		Divisional Commander inspected all Perimeter Posts of the Brigade. Training and Education as usual.	
	23/9/19.		Orders received to take over left Perimeter Post of 2nd Light Brigade at KELLUTHOR on 26th instant - 51st Bn The Rifle Brigade will furnish personnel for above. Training and Education as usual.	
	24/9/19.		Training and Education. p	
	25/9/19.		Amendment No 1 to 3rd Light Brigade Defence Instructions dated 17.7.19 issued and attached as Appendix No 1. Training and Education.	APP. No 1.
	26/9/19.		51st Bn The Rifle Brigade took over Perimeter Post at KELLERTHOR Training and Education.	
	27/9/19.		Training and Education.	
	28/9/19.		Church Parade.	
	29/9/19.		Training and Education. 53rd Bn The Rifle Brigade commenced firing Casuals for General Musketry Course and Lewis Gunners.	
	30/9/19.		Training and Education.	

Brigadier-General,
Commanding, 3rd Light Brigade.

War Diary

SECRET.

3rd LIGHT BRIGADE.

BENRATH, Germany.

25th September, 1919.

AMENDMENT NO.1 TO 3RD LIGHT BRIGADE DEFENCE INSTRUCTIONS DATED/7.7.19.

1. Page 2 is cancelled and attached table substituted.

2. Para. 6 (d) under 53rd Rifle Brigade add

    "1 Platoon on ELECTRIC WORKS near the Petrol Installation".

3. Para. 9 add "(d) Keep as many complete units in reserve as possible". Delete sentence contained in brackets at end of para.

4. Appendix "C". para 8 add

    KELLERTHOR POST is connected to H.Q. 51st Bn. The Rifle Brigade by way of HILDEN exchange and HAAN.

5. ACKNOWLEDGE.

                     Dowden
                           Captain,
           Brigade Major, 3rd Light Brigade.

To all recipients of

3rd Light Brigade Defence Instructions.

- 2 -

No. of Post.	Name.	Location.	Strength.	By whom Furnished.	REMARKS.
1.A	KELLERTHOR.	2 miles W. of HAAN.	1 Platoon.	51st R.Bde.	
1	KEMPERDICK.	1 mile S. of TRILLS.	1 Platoon.	- do -	
2	DYCKHAUS.	2 miles N. of HILDEN.	1 Platoon.	- do -	
3	REISHOLZ.	1 mile S.E. of ELLER.	2 Platoons.	- do -	
4.A	ELLER.	1 mile S. of ELLER.	1 Platoon.	52nd R.Bde.	
4	DAMSTEG.	1½ miles S. of ELLER.	1 Coy.(less 2 Platoons)	- do -	1 Platoon at 4.A 1 Platoon at REISHOLZ STATION.
5	FRIEDHOF.	½ mile S. of HALTHAUSEN.	1 Platoon.	- do -	
6	HALTHAUSEN.	HALTHAUSEN.	1 Coy.(less 1 Platoon)	- do -	
7	HIMMELGEIST.	HIMMELGEIST.	1 Company.	53rd R.Bde.	

Railway Controls are furnished as under :-

Control.	Location.	By whom furnished.	Remarks.
HILDEN.	HILDEN RLY. STATION.	Permanent.	Under 51st R.B.
REISHOLZ.	REISHOLZ RLY. STATION.	Permanent Post. Reinforced by 52nd R. Bde.	Under 52nd R.B.

PERMANENT GUARDS.

No.	Name.	Location.	Strength.	By whom Furnished.	Remarks.
8	Petrol Supply Depot.	On River 1 mile W. of BENRATH.	1 Coy.	53rd R. Bde.	

Attention is directed to Appendix "A".

Army Form C. 2118.

WAR DIARY
or
INTELLIGENCE SUMMARY

(Erase heading not required.)

HEADQUARTERS,
3rd LIGHT BRIGADE.

Instructions regarding War Diaries and Intelligence Summaries are contained in F.S. Regs., Part II. and the Staff Manual respectively. Title Pages will be prepared in manuscript.

Place	Date	Hour	Summary of Events and Information	Remarks and references to Appendices
BENRATH, Germany.	1/9/19.		Each Battalion has two Companies on duty on Perimeter Control Posts. - 51st & 52nd Bn Rif.Bde have two Companies on Training and Education. 53rd Bn Rif.Bde has two Companies firing the General Musketry Course.	
	2/9/19.		Training and Education.	
	3/9/19.		Training and Education.	
	4/9/19.		Divisional Sports.	
	5/9/19.		Training and Education - Divisional Cross Country Run and Basket Ball Final.	
	6/9/19.		Training and Education.	
	7/9/19.		Church Parade.	
	8/9/19.		Inspection of 51st & 52nd Bns. The Rifle Brigade by the Divisional Commander - After Inspection on Parade the G.O.C., saw one Company from each Battalion, at drill and one Company from each Battalion at manoeuvre - Result satisfactory.	
	9/9/19.		The usual Training and Education.	
	10/9/19.		The usual Training and Education.	
	11/9/19.		The usual Training and Education.	

Sheet 1.

Army Form C. 2118.

WAR DIARY
or
INTELLIGENCE SUMMARY
(Erase heading not required.)

Instructions regarding War Diaries and Intelligence Summaries are contained in F. S. Regs., Part II. and the Staff Manual respectively. Title Pages will be prepared in manuscript.

Place	Date	Hour	Summary of Events and Information	Remarks and references to Appendices
BENRATH, Germany.	12/9/19.		The G.O.C. in Chief visited the area and interviewed Commanding Officers. Training as usual. Orders received that in the event of the Germans not fulfilling certain conditions a mixed force would march and occupy ELBERFELD – Similar forces from all the Allies would also advance and occupy selected towns.	
	13/9/19.		Training as usual.	
	14/9/19.		Church Parade.	
	15/9/19.		Training as usual.	
	16/9/19.		51st Bn The Rifle Brigade commence firing Lewis Gun Course and Casuals for General Musketry Course. Other Units Training as usual.	
	17/9/19.		The Corps Commander visited the area and saw certain of the Control Posts. Training and Education as usual.	
	18/9/19.		Training and Education as usual.	
	19/9/19.		Training and Education.	
	20/9/19.		Training and Education.	
	21/9/19.		Church Parade.	

Sheet 2.

Army Form C. 2118.

WAR DIARY
or
INTELLIGENCE SUMMARY
(Erase heading not required.)

Instructions regarding War Diaries and Intelligence Summaries are contained in F.S. Regs., Part II. and the Staff Manual respectively. Title Pages will be prepared in manuscript.

Place	Date	Hour	Summary of Events and Information	Remarks and references to Appendices
BENRATH, Germany.	22/9/19.		Divisional Commander inspected all Perimeter Posts of the Brigade. Training and Education as usual.	
	23/9/19.		Orders received to take over left Perimeter Post of 2nd Light Brigade at KELLUTHOR on 26th instant – 51st Bn The Rifle Brigade will furnish personnel for above. Training and Education as usual.	
	24/9/19.		Training and Education. p	
	25/9/19.		Amendment No 1 to 3rd Light Brigade Defence Instructions dated 17.7.19 issued and attached as Appendix No 1. Training and Education.	APP. No 1.
	26/9/19.		51st Bn The Rifle Brigade took over Perimeter Post at KELLERTHOR Training and Education.	
	27/9/19.		Training and Education.	
	28/9/19.		Church Parade.	
	29/9/19.		Training and Education. 53rd Bn The Rifle Brigade commenced firing Casuals for General Musketry Course and Lewis Gunners.	
	30/9/19.		Training and Education.	

Brigadier-General,
Commanding, 3rd Light Brigade.

War Diary

SECRET.

3rd LIGHT BRIGADE.

BENRATH, Germany.   25th September, 1919.

AMENDMENT NO.1 TO 3RD LIGHT BRIGADE DEFENCE INSTRUCTIONS DATED/7.7.19.

1. Page 2 is cancelled and attached table substituted.

2. Para. 6 (d) under 53rd Rifle Brigade add

    "1 Platoon on ELECTRIC WORKS near the Petrol Installation".

3. Para. 9 add "(d) Keep as many complete units in reserve as possible"

    Delete sentence contained in brackets at end of para.

4. Appendix "C". para 8 add

    KELLERTHOR POST is connected to H.Q. 51st Bn. The Rifle Brigade by way of HILDEN exchange and HAAN.

5. ACKNOWLEDGE.

                                                    Captain,
                                Brigade Major, 3rd Light Brigade.

To all recipients of

    3rd Light Brigade Defence Instructions.

No. of Post.	Name.	Location.	Strength.	By whom Furnished.	REMARKS.
1.A	KELLERTHOR.	2 miles W. of HAAN.	1 Platoon.	51st R.Bde.	
1.	KEMPERDICK.	1 mile S. of TRILLS.	1 Platoon.	- do -	
2	DICKHAUS.	2 miles N. of HILDEN.	1 Platoon.	- do -	
3	REISHOLZ.	1 mile S.E. of ELLER.	2 Platoons.	- do -	
4.A	ELLER.	1 mile S. of ELLER.	1 Platoon.	52nd R.Bde.	
4	DAMSTEG.	1½ miles S. of ELLER.	1 Coy.(less 2 Platoons)	- do -	1 Platoon at 4.A 1 Platoon at REISHOLZ STATION.
5	FRIEDHOF.	½ mile S. of HALTHAUSEN.	1 Platoon.	- do -	
6	HALTHAUSEN.	HALTHAUSEN.	1 Coy.(less 1 Platoon)	- do -	
7	HIMMELGEIST.	HIMMELGEIST.	1 Company.	53rd R.Bde.	

Railway Controls are furnished as under :-

Control.	Location.	By whom furnished.	Remarks.
HILDEN.	HILDEN RLY. STATION.	Permanent.	Under 51st R.B.
REISHOLZ.	REISHOLZ RLY. STATION.	Permanent Post. Reinforced by 52nd R. Bde.	Under 52nd R.B.

PERMANENT GUARDS.

No.	Name.	Location.	Strength.	By whom Furnished.	Remarks.
8	Petrol Supply Depot.	On River 1 mile W. of BENRATH.	1 Coy.	53rd R. Bde.	

Attention is drawn directed to Appendix "A".

Army Form C. 2118.

WAR DIARY
or
INTELLIGENCE SUMMARY

(Erase heading not required.)

Place	Date	Hour	Summary of Events and Information	Remarks and references to Appendices
BENRATH.	OCTOBER.1919.			
	1		Brigade Signal Section under Lieut. Mc IVOR withdrawn from Brigade to Divisional Headquarters. Brigade to maintain communication with personnel drawn from Units of the Brigade. Casuals of 53rd Bn. The Rifle Brigade and the 5rench Mortar Battery firing the General Musketry Course. Lewis Gunners of 53rd Bn. The Rifle Brigade firing Lewis Gun Course. Remainder of the Brigade not on duty on Perimeter Posts, Permanent Guards, etc., undergoing the usual Training and Education. 157th Field Company withdrawn from the Brigade Group. All Field Companies of the Division concentrated at WALD under C.R.E.	
	2-4		Training and Education as usual.	
	5		Church Parades.	
	6-7		Training and Education.	
	8		Orders received that the BELGIANS would take over from the Brigade on 15th instant. INformation received as to the ultimate composition of the Rhine Forces. Two Battalions of the Brigade (51st and 52nd Bns. The Rifle Brigade) are to be retained. Conference of Commanding Officers and Adjutants at Brigade Headquarters on re-organization consequent on above. Training and Education as usual.	
	9		Orders received to despatch two Companies to Rhine Army Concentration Camp for duty. Training as usual.	
	10		One Company made up to 150 retainable men from 52nd Bn. The Rifle Brigade and one Company made up to 100 retainable men from 53rd Bn. The Rifle Brigade proceeded to Rhine Army Concentration Camp by lorry for duty. Probable duration of stay 3 to 4 weeks.	

Army Form C. 2118.

WAR DIARY
or
INTELLIGENCE SUMMARY
(Erase heading not required.)

Instructions regarding War Diaries and Intelligence Summaries are contained in F. S. Regs., Part II. and the Staff Manual respectively. Title Pages will be prepared in manuscript.

Place	Date	Hour	Summary of Events and Information	Remarks and references to Appendices
BENRATH.	OCTOBER, 1919. Sheet 2.			
	10		The above two companies were made up to strength with all available men from the Battalions concerned. Guard on PETROL INSTALLATION reduced to ½ Company and HIMMELGEIST POST reduced to 3 Platoons. The 3 released Platoons withdrawn to Headquarters, 53rd Bn. The Rifle Brigade, BENRATH.	
	11		Conference at Brigade Headquarters of Commanding Officers and Officers Commanding the FRENCH Regiment taking over the area to arrange details of relief.	
	12		Church Parades.	
			Further conference with FRENCH Officers regarding the taking over as previous arrangements have now been changed and only one Battalion instead of two are taking over. Brigade Order No. 7 issued.	
	13		Billeting party from FRENCH Regiment arrived. Staff Captain proceeded to OPLADEN to billet the Brigade. Orders received that the Railway Control Posts at HILDEN and REISHOLZ will not be handed over to the FRENCH.	
			All orders regarding the relief of the Brigade by the FRENCH are postponed indefinitely.	
	14		Some Education. No men available for training.	
	14-17		Guard on PETROL INSTALLATION withdrawn as establishment now handed over to Civilian Firm.	
	18		Orders received that the 53rd Bn. The Rifle Brigade will be disbanded at once. Disbandment to be completed by 21st instant. All personnel of 53rd Bn. The Rifle Brigade to be posted to 51st and 52nd Bns. The Rifle Brigade. The Trench Mortar Battery will also be disbanded and personnel reposted to their respective Battalions. Disbandment to be completed by 21st inst.	

Army Form C. 2118.

WAR DIARY
or
INTELLIGENCE SUMMARY

(Erase heading not required.)

Instructions regarding War Diaries and Intelligence Summaries are contained in F.S. Regs., Part II. and the Staff Manual respectively. Title Pages will be prepared in manuscript.

Place	Date	Hour	Summary of Events and Information	Remarks and references to Appendices
BENRATH.	OCTOBER, 1919. Sheet 3.			
	19		Church Parades.	
	20		Disbandment of 53rd Bn. The Rifle Brigade and Trench Mortar Battery being carried out.	
	21		Garrisons of Perimeter Posts re-organized. The 52nd Bn. The Rifle Brigade took over HIMMELGEIST POST from 53rd Bn. The Rifle Brigade who are being disbanded.	
			53rd Bn. The Rifle Brigade and 3rd L.T.M. Battery disbanded and personnel posted to 51st and 52nd Bns. The Rifle Brigade. Orders received that Brigadier General H. B. KENNEDY, C.M.G., D.S.O. would proceed and take over Command of the 1st Light Brigade and that Brigadier General P. A. M. CURRIE, C.M.G., D.S.O. would assume Command of 3rd Light Brigade on his return from leave about 28th instant. Also that Captain C. H. DOWDEN, D.S.O., M.C., K.R.R.C. would proceed to ENGLAND as surplus to establishment as soon as duties of Brigade Major, 3rd Light Brigade were handed over to Captain G. E. M. WHITTUCK, M.C. at present Brigade Major, 2nd Light Brigade. 2nd Light Brigade would be disbanded about 28th instant.	
	22-25		Training and Education as usual.	
	26		Church Parade.	
	27		51st and 52nd Bns. The Rifle Brigade carried out rehearsals of "Precautionary Measure" to be taken in the event of a Civil Disturbance. Everything correct.	
	28		Brigadier General H. B. KENNEDY, C.M.G., D.S.O. left to assume Command of 1st Light Brigade. Brigadier General, R. A. M. CURRIE, C.M.G., D.S.O. arrived and assumed Command of 3rd Light Brigade vice Brigadier General KENNEDY. Captain G. E. M. WHITTUCK, M.C. arrived to assume duties of Brigade Major, 3rd Light Brigade, vice Captain C. H. DOWDEN, D.S.O., M.C. who is to proceed to ENGLAND on 31st instant after handing over duties to Captain WHITTUCK, M.C.	
			Orders received that the FRENCH would relieve Brigade about 2nd or 3rd November.	

Army Form C. 2118.

WAR DIARY
or
INTELLIGENCE SUMMARY

(Erase heading not required.)

Instructions regarding War Diaries and Intelligence Summaries are contained in F.S. Regs., Part II and the Staff Manual respectively. Title Pages will be prepared in manuscript.

Place	Date	Hour	Summary of Events and Information	Remarks and references to Appendices
BENRATH.	OCTOBER, 1919.		Sheet 4.	
	28		Training and Education as usual.	
			Two Companies rejoined Brigade from Rhine Army Concentration Camp.	
	29.		Orders received that 3rd Light Brigade would relieve the 1st Light Brigade on being relieved by the FRENCH in present area on 2nd-3rd November.	
			Usual Education and Training and re-organization of Companies returned from COLOGNE.	
	30		Orders received that the FRENCH would not take over the Brigade Area. One BELGIAN Battalion ordered to take over BENRATH and Posts in its immediate vicinity. Confirmation not received.	
			Lieut. Colonel The Hon. R. BRAND, C.M.G., D.S.O. took over Command of the 51st Bn. The Rifle Brigade	
			Orders received for 3rd Light Brigade Headquarters to be retained with the Rhine Garrison as 2nd Garrison Brigade.	
	31		Cadre of 53rd Bn. The Rifle Brigade disbanded at 1200 hours. Orders received that Captain WILKINS, D.S.O., M.C. would join the Brigade forthwith as Staff Captain vice Captain T.K. NEWBIGGING, M.C. to be Staff Captain, 1st Light Brigade.	

Commanding 3rd Light Brigade.
Brigadier General,

War Diary

SECRET.

Copy No. 25

3rd LIGHT BRIGADE.

ADMINISTRATIVE INSTRUCTIONS NO.1.

(To accompany 3rd Light Brigade Order No.8.)

1. LORRIES.

Lorries as under will report at H.Q. of Units

Unit.	Lorries.	Date.	Hour.	May be used for:-
51st Bn Rifle Bde.	1.	3/11/19	0800	2 Journeys.
52nd Bn Rifle Bde.	6.	2/11/19	0800	do.
3rd Light Bde H.Q.	1.	3/11/19	0600	3 Journeys.
51st Bn Rifle Bde.	2.	3/11/19	0800	2 Journeys.
51st Bn Rifle Bde.	1	4/11/19	0600	(if required).

2. TRAM ARRANGEMENTS.

Reference Table "C" issued with 3rd Light Brigade Order No.8.

Trams leaving HILDEN at 0900 hours and BENRATH at 1000 hours will each have 1 additional wagon attached.

These additional wagons will be used for the conveyance of blankets and kit bags and will be at HILDEN and BENRATH 2 hours previous to scheduled time of departure, for loading.

A loading party will be provided by battalions concerned for the changing of trams at OHLIGS.

3. HANDING OVER.

All requisitioned stores with the exception of those mentioned in para. 4 taken over from Lowland Division, in addition to those since requisitioned by units of this Brigade, will be handed over to Burgomasters concerned.

Handing over of stores will be carried out in accordance with Appendix "B" to Light Division Instructions No.1. (Copy attached)

All Dumps of requisitioned Stores will be reported to D.A.D.O.S. Light Division Reference D.R.O.1074 dated 14th October 1919.

4. STORES TO BE TAKEN TO NEW AREA.

The following requisitioned stores will be taken by units to new area:-

(a) Paillasses and Pillows (where required) - empty. All straw to be carefully burned.

(b) Knives, forks, spoons, plates etc., sufficient to complete each man.

(c) Sentry boxes (not more than two per battalion).

5. ORDNANCE.

Ordnance stores other than Mobilization Equipment - i.e. tents, latrine buckets etc., will be returned to D.A.D.O.S. under battalion arrangements, previous to the move.

6. BILLETING.

Billeting parties will precede battalions, under battalion arrangements,:-

Billets will be taken over as follows :-

3rd Light Bde H.Q. from	1st Light Brigade H.Q.
51st Bn Rifle Bde. from	13th K.R.R.C.
52nd Bn Rifle Brigade	(Perimeter Posts from 20th K.R.R.C (SOLINGEN Billets from 13 K.R.R.C.

7. SUPPLIES.

On 1st November units will refill for consumption on 3rd November 1919.

There will be no refilling on 2nd November. Units will consume the extra days rations now on hand on that date.

Refilling on 3rd November will take place as at present.

[signature] TK Newbigging

Captain.
Staff Captain.
3rd Light Brigade.

Copies to :-

1. File.
2. War Diary.
3. G.O.C.
4. Brigade Major.
5. Staff Captain.
6. Staff Captain. (Civil).
7. 51st Bn The Rifle Brigade.
8. 52nd Bn The Rifle Brigade.
9. H.Q. Div. Train.
10. Light Division "G"
11. Light Division "Q"
12. P.R.O. 3rd Light Brigade.
13. 1st Light Brigade.

SECRET.

Copy No. 2A

3RD LIGHT BRIGADE.

30/10/19.

ORDER NO. 8.

1. CANCELLATION.

Brigade Order No. 7 dated 12/10/19 is cancelled.

2. RELIEF.

(a)   The area now occupied by the 3rd Light Brigade, plus certain posts in the 1st Light Brigade Area now held by 18th K.R.R.C. will be taken over by the 171st FRENCH Regiment on 2nd and 3rd November, 1919.

On relief the 3rd Light Brigade will move to the SOLINGEN-OHLIGS-WALD Area and relieve the 1st Light Brigade as shown on Table 'B'.

(b)   All perimeter Posts of 3rd Light Brigade will be relieved on the afternoon of the 2nd November in accordance with Table 'A' attached. On relief garrisons of Posts etc., will rejoin Units. Railway Control Posts in present area will not be relieved or withdrawn but will remain in situ.
These Posts will come under the direct orders of the Inter Allied Railway Sub-Commission, on 3/11/19.

(c)   The remainder of the Area will be taken over on the 3rd Nov.

(d)   Table 'C' shows tram accommodation.

(e)   Completion of relief of Perimeter Posts will be notified to these Headquarters.

3. GUIDES.

Units will furnish guides to be at the Ferry HIMMELGEIST at 1100 hours as under:-

(a)   2nd November, 1919.
   (i)   **18th K.R.R.C.**

One French speaking Officer and one guide from each post to be relieved.

   (ii)   **51st Bn. The Rifle Brigade.**

One French speaking Officer and one guide from each post to be relieved.

   (iii)   **52nd Bn. The Rifle Brigade.**

One French speaking Officer and one guide from each post to be relieved.

-2-

    (b)   <u>3rd November, 1919.</u>

        (i)   <u>18th K.R.R.C.</u>

              One Officer guide to meet troops for HAAN.

        (ii)   <u>51st Bn. The Rifle Brigade.</u>

              One Officer and two N.C.Os. guides to conduct Battalion Headquarters and Companies to HILDEN.

        (iii) <u>52nd Bn. The Rifle Brigade.</u>

              One Officer and two N.C.Os. to guide Battalion Headquarters and troops to BENRATH.
              One Officer to guide Regimental Headquarters to BENRATH.

    (c)   Officers in charge of guides will be responsible that the guides take correct parties and that they proceed by the trams detailed.

4.   <u>REAR PARTIES.</u>

    (I)   Each Battalion will leave the following personnel with the relieving Unit for a period of 48 hours:-

        (a)   Battalion Headquarters:
              One Officer who can speak French and is well acquainted with Battalion Billets, etc.

        (b)   Companies employed on Control Posts:- One Officer.

        (c)   Each Post:, One Sergeant or Corporal.

    (II)   The Officers left behind as above, will ensure that any Military Equipment such as telephones etc-, that may have been left behind with the relieving Unit as a temporary measure are brought away when they leave to rejoin their Unit at the expiration of 48 hours.

    (III) Units leaving personnel as above, will be responsible for rationing, and any transport that may be necessary to with draw it.

    (IV)   1st Light Brigade are leaving a proportion of Officers and N.C.Os. on Railway Control and Perimeter Posts for 24 hours after relief.

5.   <u>ADVANCE PARTIES.</u>

    (a)   A French advance party to arrange accommodation etc., will arrive on the morning of the 1st November and will be sent on to Units concerned.

        Units will arrange to hand over billets etc., and to accommodate and feed billeting parties as under:-

              (i)   HAAN.   18th K.R.R.C.

              (ii) HILDEN.   51st Bn. The Rifle Brigade.

              (iii) BENRATH.   52nd Bn. The Rifle Brigade.

-3-

    (b)   Units will send on Advance Parties to the 1st Light Brigade Area to carry out necessary reconnaissance and arrange accommodation etc., on November 1st.

6. **CIVIL ADMINISTRATION.**

    (a)   Civil Administration of the present area will be handed over to the FRENCH on the 3rd November, 1919.

    (b)   The Civil Administration of the present 1st Light Brigade area will be taken over by the 3rd Light Brigade at 1400 hours on 3/11/19.

7. **DEFENCE SCHEMES.**

    All Defence Schemes, information as to training areas, Ranges etc., will be handed over to relieving Units. 52nd Bn. The Rifle Brigade will hand over the Brigade Rifle Range and all instructions relating to safety connected therewith.

    Orders for Perimeter Posts and Local Defence Schemes will be translated into French before handing over.

    Defence Schemes, Training Areas, etc., will be taken over by Units from Battalions of 1st Light Brigade on relief.

    A rehearsal of local defence schemes will be carried out by Units within 24 hours of relief and result reported to Brigade Headquarters.

8. **AREA STORES.**

    Instructions regarding area stores etc., will be issued separately.

9. **GENERAL.**

    All further arrangements regarding the relief and move will be made by O.C. Units concerned.

10. **MOVE COMPLETE.**

    Completion of move to the new area together with location of Headquarters will be wired to Brigade Headquarters as early as possible.

11. **COMMAND.**

    (a) Command of the present 3rd Light Brigade Area will pass from G.O.C. 3rd Light Brigade to G.O.C. FRENCH Troops at 1200 hours on 3rd November, 1919.

    (b) The 18th K.R.R.C. are remaining in the OHLIGS-WALD Area and will come under the Tactical Orders of G.O.C. 3rd Light Brigade at 1400 hours on 3/11/19.

    (c) Command of 1st Light Brigade Area will pass to G.O.C. 3rd Light Brigade at 1400 hours on 3/11/19.

12. **ACKNOWLEDGE.**

Captain,
Brigade Major,
3rd Light Brigade.

Copies to:-

1. File.
2. War Diary.
3. G.O.C.
4. Brigade Major.
5. Staff Captain.
6. Staff Captain (Civil).
7. Brigade Signals.
8. Brigade I.O.
9. 81st Bn. The Rifle Brigade.
10. 82nd Bn. The Rifle Brigade.
11. 18th K.R.R.C.
12. 1st Light Brigade.
13. Light Division "Q"
14. Light Division "G"
15.)
16.)
17.) 171st French Regiment.
18.) (through Light Division).
19.)
20.)
21. P.R.O.
22. No. 4 Company Train.
23.)
24.)
25.)
26.) Spare.
27.)
28.)
29.)
30.)

TABLE "A".

ARRANGEMENTS FOR RELIEF OF POSTS BY FRENCH.

Post to be taken over.	Strength.	Furnished by.	To be relieved by.
LOOP POST. / GRUITEN POST.	1 Section.	18th. K.R.R.C.	FRENCH REGT.
H.P. POST. / HAHNENMUHLE POST.	1 Section.	18th. K.R.R.C.	FRENCH REGT.
KEMPERDICK POST.	½ Section.	51st. Rifle Bde.	FRENCH REGT.
DICKHAUS POST.	½ Section.	51st. Rifle Bde.	FRENCH REGT.
REISHOLZ POST.	1 Section.	51st. Rifle Bde.	1/171ST. FRENCH REGT.
DAMSTEN POST. / ELLER POST.	1 Section.	52nd. Rifle Bde.	1/171ST. FRENCH REGT.
FRIEDHOF POST.	½ Section.	52nd. Rifle Bde.	1/171ST. FRENCH REGT.
HOLTHAUSEN POST.	1½ Sections.	52nd. Rifle Bde.	1/171ST. FRENCH REGT.
HIMMELGEIST.	½ Section.	52nd. Rifle Bde.	1/171ST. FRENCH REGT.

LOCATION OF FRENCH ON COMPLETION OF RELIEF.

Formation or Unit.	Location.	Remarks.
1/ H.Qrs. 171st. French Regt.	BENRATH.	2 Companies in BENRATH. 2 Companies on Post.
H.Qrs. 1/171st. French Regt.	HILDEN.	2 Companies HILDEN. 1 Company Post HILDEN. 1 Company HAAN and Posts.
H.Qrs. 171st. French Regt.	BENRATH.	

TABLE "B"

Arrangements for relief of 1st. Light Brigade by 3rd. Light Brigade.

Date.	Unit.	From.	To.	Relieving.	Remarks.
3/11/19.	1 Coy. & 1 Platoon 51st. R.B.	HILDEN.	Perimeter Posts new Area.	Railway Control & Perimeter Posts of 13th.K.R.R.C.	By Tram from HILDEN to GRAFRATH.
3/11/19.	51st.R.B. (less troops as above)	HILDEN.	SOLINGEN via OHLIGS.	13th. K.R.R.C.	By March route - One tram will be provided to carry packs & steel helmets.
	52nd. R. Brigade (less 2 Coys.)	BENRATH.	SOLINGEN.	20th.K.R.R.C.	By March route etc To take over accommodation vacated by K.R.R.C. on 25/10/19. ―18th
	2 Coys. 52nd.R. Brigade.	BENRATH.	Perimeter Posts.	Railway Control & Perimeter posts from 20th.K.R.R.C.	By Tram to GRAFRATH.

Location of 3rd. Light Brigade on Completion of Relief.

Formation of Unit.	Location.	Remarks.
H.Q. 3rd. Light Bde.	WALD.	H.Q. now occupied by 1st. Light Brigade.
51st.Rifle Brigade.	SOLINGEN. (One Company & 1 platoon on Perimeter now held by 13th. K.R.R.C.)	H.Q. now occupied by 13th. K.R.R.C.
52nd.Rifle Brigade.	SOLINGEN.(2 Companies on Perimeter now held by 20th. K.R.R.C.)	H.Q. that was occupied by 18th. K.R.R.C. on 22/10/19.
19th.K.R.R.C. (attached).	OHLIGS.	Under tactical orders of G.O.C.3rd.Light Brigade

SERIAL "C".

TRAM ARRANGEMENTS.

Date.	Area to be at:-	Time.	To proceed to:-	Numbers for which accommodation is required.	Change at:-	Proceeding to:-	Unit for which required.	Remarks.
2/11/19.	HILDEN.	10.00 hrs.	CHAPLAIN.	140.	OHLIGS.	Perimeter Posts etc.	51st.R.B.	
2/11/19.	MOLLHAUSE.	16.00	HAAN.	100.	BENRATH & HILDEN.	LOOP & HP POSTS.	French Regt.	
"	do.	do.	MILLER.	140.	AMRATH.	KIRPERICK & BLUHRATE PROV.	French Regt.	
3/11/19.	HILDEN.	09.00	SOLINGEN.	One tram to carry Steel Helmets and Box Respirators. 320 and 1 tram for	OHLIGS.	SOLINGEN.	51st.R.B.	
"	BENRATH.	10.00	SOLINGEN.	Steel Helmets & Box Respirators.	OHLIGS.	Perimeter Posts etc.	52nd.R.B.	
"	MOLLHAUSE.	12.00	HAAN.	60	BENRATH & MILLER.	HAAN.	French Regt.	
"	do	do	HILDEN.	400	BENRATH.	HILDEN.	French Regt.	
"	do	do	BENRATH.	700	BENRATH.	Regt. H.--171 French Regt. Bn.H.Q. & 2 Co.s.	French Regt.	

Remainder of Brigade will move by March Route under Unit's arrangements. Troops marching will not carry Steel Helmets or Box Respirators. These go by tram.

War Diary

S E C R E T.

3rd LIGHT BRIGADE.

BENRATH, Germany.   24th October, 1919.

**AMENDMENT NO. 2 TO 3RD LIGHT BRIGADE
DEFENCE INSTRUCTIONS DATED 17.7.19.**

1.   On page 2 item Post No.7 for

       "2 Platoons" read "1 Platoon".

2.   Para. 6 (d) will be amended to read as under :-

(d) The following guards will be mounted :-

             51st Bn. The Rifle Brigade.

1 Section on HILDEN TELEPHONE EXCHANGE.

             52nd Bn. The Rifle Brigade.

(i) 2 Platoons on the BENRATH ELECTRICAL WORKS.

(ii) 1 Platoon (less 2 sections) on the ARMY PETROL INSTALLATION.

(iii) 2 Sections on BENRATH WATER-WORKS.

(iv) 1 Section on BRIGADE HEADQUARTERS AND TELEPHONE OFFICE.

(v) 1 Section on BENRATH TELEPHONE EXCHANGE.

                                                     Captain,

                      Brigade Major, 3rd Light Brigade.

To all recipients of
3rd Light Brigade Defence Instructions.

3rd LIGHT BRIGADE.

BENRATH, Germany.   19th October, 1919.

AMENDMENT NO. 2 TO 3RD LIGHT BRIGADE
DEFENCE INSTRUCTIONS DATED 17.7.19.

1. Page 2 is cancelled and the attached "Page 2" substituted.

2. In para. 5 (ii) (b) erase the word "SENIOR".

3. Cancel para. 6 (d) and substitute

   (d) The following guards will be mounted :-

   51st RIFLE BRIGADE.

   1 section on HILDEN TELEPHONE EXCHANGE.

   52nd RIFLE BRIGADE.

   1 section on Brigade H.Q. and Signal Office.
   1 section on BENRATH Civil Telephone Exchange.
   1 Platoon (less 2 sections) on Army Petrol Installation on the Rhine Bank.
   2 sections on BENRATH Electrical Works, near the Petrol Installation on the Rhine.

4. ACKNOWLEDGE.

                                            Captain,
                        Brigade Major, 3rd Light Brigade.

To all recipients of
3rd Light Brigade Defence Instructions.

No. of Post.	Name.	Location.	Strength.	By whom furnished.	Remarks
1.A	KELLERTHOR.	2 miles W. of HAAN.	1 Platoon.	51st R.B.	
1	KEMPERDICK.	1 mile S. of TRILLS.	1 Platoon.	-do-	
2	DICKHAUS.	2 miles N. of HILDEN.	1 Platoon.	-do-	
3	REISHOLZ POST.	1 mile S.E. of ELLER.	2 Platoons.	-do-	
4.A	ELLER.	1 mile S. of ELLER.	Furnished from REISHOLZ STN.	52nd R.B.	
4	DER STEG.	1½ miles S. of ELLER.	1 Platoon.	-do-	
5	FRIEDHOF.	½ mile S. of HOLTHAUSEN.	1 Platoon.	-do-	
6	HOLTHAUSEN.	HOLTHAUSEN.	2 Platoons.	-do-	
7	HIMMELGEIST.	HIMMELGEIST.	2 Platoons.	-do-	

Railway Controls are furnished as under :-

Control.	Location.	Strength.	By whom furnished.	Remarks.
HILDEN.	HILDEN RLY. STATION.	1 Platoon.	51st R.B.	
REISHOLZ.	REISHOLZ RLY. STATION.	2 Platoons.	52nd R.B.	Furnishes ELLER POST.

Attention is directed to Appendix "A".

War Diary

SECRET.

3rd LIGHT BRIGADE.

TINTRAIL, Germany.   14th October, 1918.

1.   All moves and reliefs ordered in 3rd Light Brigade Order No. 7 are postponed indefinitely.

2.   ACKNOWLEDGE.

                                        [signature]
                                                    Captain,
                        Brigade Major, 3rd Light Brigade.

To all recipients of
    3rd Light Brigade Order No. 7.

War Diary

SECRET.

Copy No. 2.

3rd LIGHT BRIGADE.

ADMINISTRATIVE INSTRUCTIONS No. 1.

(To accompany 3rd Light Brigade Order No. 7.)

---

1. **LORRIES.**

    Lorries as under will report at Headquarters of Units on the evening of 14th inst.
    Brigade H.Q.   5.   (Includes 1 for T..Bty.)
    Each Battalion.   3.
    No.4. Coy. Train.   1.
    Each lorry may be used for second journey if required.

2. **HANDING OVER.**

    All requisitioned stores with the exception of those mentioned in para. 3. taken over from Lowland Division, in addition to those since requisitioned by units, of this Brigade will be handed over to relieving units.
    Receipts for stores in billets etc., not being taken over by the French will be obtained from the Burgomasters concerned.
    Handing over certificates and receipts for requisitioned stores will be rendered to reach Brigade Headquarters on the day of the move.
    The pro-forma issued with 3rd Light Brigade No.G.78 of the 8th inst., (To units of Brigade Group only) will be used for this purpose.

3. **STORES TO BE TAKEN TO NEW AREA.**

    The following requisitioned stores will be taken by units to new area:-
    (a) Paillasses and Pillows - empty. All straw to be carefully burned.
    (b) Knives, forks, spoons, plates etc., sufficient to complete each man, including those temporarily detached.
    (c) Sentry boxes. (Not more than two per unit.)

4. **ORDNANCE.**

    Ordnance Stores other than Mobilization Equipment - i.e. tents, latrine buckets, etc., will be collected by units at their Headquarters on morning of 14th inst., from where they will be removed under arrangements to be made by Brigade Headquarters.
    In the event of these stores not being collected before the unit moves a small guard will be left and rationed for the 14th inst.

5. **BEDS.**

    Beds sufficient to equip each man in new area will be collected from D.A.D.O.S. on the 14th inst., under instructions to be issued later,

SECRET.

-2-

6. BILLETING.

(a) Billeting parties of 51st Bn. The Rifle Brigade will precede the Battalion under arrangements to be made by O.C. Battalion.

(b) Billeting parties from all other units will proceed to OPLADEN on the 14th inst., and will be accommodated for the night 14/15th October under arrangements being made by Civil Administration Staff OPLADEN, to whom they will report on arrival.

7. SUPPLIES.

Units will refill twice on the 14th inst.,
Second Refilling will be at 1400 hours and Supply wagons will be used.
Baggage and Supply wagons will be horsed by No. 4. Coy. Train, and will march with their own units, rejoining No. 4. Coy. Train on completion of move.

8. ACKNOWLEDGE.

Captain,
Staff Captain, 3rd Light Brigade.

Copies to:-

1. File.
2. War Diary.
3. G.O.C.
4. Brigade Major.
5. Staff Captain.
6. Staff Captain. (Civil).
7. 51st Bn. The Rifle Bde.
8. 52nd Bn. The Rifle Bde.
9. 53rd Bn. The Rifle Bde.
10. 3rd Light Trench Mortar Battery.
11. No. 4. Coy. Train.
12. Light Division. "G".
13. Light Division. "Q".
14. P.R.O. 3rd Light Bde.

War Diary.

SECRET.
Copy No. 2

3rd LIGHT BRIGADE.

O R D E R No. 7.

12th October 1919.

1. **RELIEF.**

    (a) The area now occupied by the 3rd Light Brigade, plus certain posts in the 2nd Light Brigade Area now held by 12th Royal Irish Rifles will be taken over by the 171st FRENCH Regiment on the 14th and 15th inst.

    (b) All Perimeter Posts and Railway Controls will be relieved on the afternoon of the 14th inst., in accordance with Table "A" attached. On relief garrisons of posts etc., will rejoin units.

    (c) The remainder of the area will be taken over on the 15th inst.

    (d) Table "B" shows tram accommodation for relieving troops.

    (e) Completion of relief to be notified to these Headquarters.

2. **GUIDES.**

    Battalions will furnish guides to be at Ferry, HIMMELGEIST as under:-

    (i)   12th R.I.Rifles.
        (a) One French speaking Officer to guide H.Q. of Coy., and one section to HAAN.
        (b) One N.C.O. from each Post to guide relieving units.

    (ii) 51st Rifle Brigade.
        (a) One French speaking Officer to guide H.Q. of Coy., and one section to HILDEN.
        (b) One N.C.O. from each Post to guide relieving units.

    (iii) 52nd Rifle Brigade.
        One guide from each Post to be taken over. Guides to be under a French speaking Officer.

    (iv) 53rd Rifle Brigade.
        (a) One French speaking Officer to guide Battalion H.Q. and one N.C.O. to guide each of the two Company H.Q. to BENRATH.
        (b) One N.C.O. from each Post to guide relieving units.

    (v)   Officers in charge of guides will be responsible that guides take off correct parties, and that they proceed by the trams detailed in Table "B".

3. **REAR PARTIES.**

    (1) Each Battalion will leave the following personnel with the relieving unit for a period of 48 hours:-

        (a) Battalion Headquarters (except 52nd Bn.Rifle Bde):-
            One Officer who can speak French and is well acquainted with Battalion billets etc.

        (b) Companies employed on Control Posts and Railway Controls :- One Officer.

        (c) Each Post:- One Officer or Sergeant.

(ii).........

3. REAR PARTIES. (Contd).

   (ii)   The Officers left behind as above, will ensure that any Military Equipment such as Telephones that may have been left behind with the relieving unit as a temporary measure are brought away when they leave to rejoin their unit at the expiration of 48 hours.

   (iii) Units leaving personnel as above, will be responsible for rationing, and any transport that may be necessary to withdraw it.

4. ADVANCE PARTIES.

   An Advance Party of 1 Officer and 12 O.Rs to arrange accommodation etc., will arrive on the morning of the 13th inst., and will be sent on to units concerned.
   Units as under will arrange to hand over billets and to accommodate and feed billetting parties:-

   (a) HAAN.   12th Royal Irish Rifles.

   (b) HILDEN.   51st Bn. The Rifle Brigade.

   (c) BENRATH.   53rd Bn. The Rifle Brigade.

5. MOVE.

   On completion of relief as above, the Brigade Group will march to the area OPLADEN - SCHLEBUSCH - LEICHLINGEN in accordance with March Table "D" attached.
   Distances on the march will be maintained as laid down in Para 1. "Notes on March Discipline".

6. CIVIL ADMINISTRATION.

   (a) Civil Administration of the present Area will be handed over to the FRENCH on the 15th inst.

   (b) The Civil Administration of the Area OPLADEN - SCHLEBUSCH - LEICHLINGEN will be taken over by 3rd Light Brigade.

   (c) Further instructions under this heading will be issued as soon as known.

7. DEFENCE SCHEMES.

   All Defence Schemes, information as to Training Areas, Ranges etc., will be handed over to relieving units. 53rd Bn. The Rifle Brigade will hand over the Brigade Rifle Range and all instructions relating to safety connected therewith.

8. **AREA STORES.**

   Instructions regarding area stores etc. will be issued separately.

9. **GENERAL.**

   All further arrangements regarding the relief and move will be made by O.C. Units concerned.

10. **MOVE COMPLETE.**

    Completion of move to the new area together with location of Headquarters will be wired to Brigade Headquarters as early as possible.

    ACKNOWLEDGE.

    E. K. Dowden
    Captain,
    Brigade Major, 3rd Light Brigade.

Copies to :-
1. File.
2. War Diary.
3. G.O.C.
4. Brigade Major.
5. Staff Captain.
6. Staff Captain (Civil).
7. Brigade Signals.
8. Brigade I.O.
9. 51st Bn. The Rifle Brigade.
10. 52nd Bn. The Rifle Brigade.
11. 53rd Bn. The Rifle Brigade.
12. 3rd Light T..B.
13. No. 4 Coy. Train.
14. 12th Royal Irish Rifles.
15. 2nd Light Brigade.
16. Light Division "B".
17. Light Division "Q"
18.)
19.) 171st French Regiment.
20.)
21.) (through Light Division).
22.)
23.)
24. P.M.O.

TABLE "A".

ARRANGEMENTS FOR RELIEF.

Posts to be taken over.	Strength of Relief.	Now furnished by.	Relieved by.	Remarks.
LOOP POST. GRUITEN POST.	1 Sect.	10th R.I.R.	171 French Regt.	1st Coy. H.Q. and one Section in HAAN.
ELP POST. MAHNERTMUHLE POST.	1 Sect.	10th R.I.R.	171 French Regt.	
KEMPERDICK POST.	½ Sect.	51st R.Bde.	171 French Regt.	2nd Coy. H.Q. and one Section in HILDEN.
DICKHAUS POST.	½ Sect.	51st R.Bde.	171 French Regt.	
HILDEN STATION.	1 Sect.	51st R.Bde.	171 French Regt.	
REISHOLZ POST.	½ Sect.	51st R.Bde.	171 French Regt.	3rd Coy. H.Q. and one Section in BENRATH.
REISHOLZ STATION & ELLER POST.	1½ Sects.	52nd R.Bde.	171 French Regt.	
DAMSTEG POST.	½ Sect.	52nd R.Bde.	171 French Regt.	Battalion H.Q. 4th Coy. H.Q. and ½ Sect. in BENRATH.
FRIEDHOF POST.	½ Sect.	52nd R.Bde.	171 French Regt.	
HOLTHAUSEN POST.	1 Sect.	52nd R.Bde.	171 French Regt.	
HIMMELGEIST POST.	½ Sect.	53rd R.Bde.	171 French Regt.	

(a) KELLERTHOR Post will not be relieved. O.C. 51st R.Bde. will close the road and withdraw the garrison at 14.00 hours on 14th inst.
(b) The Guard at the PETROL INSTALLATION will not be relieved but will be withdrawn at 09.00 hours on 15th inst., when command passes to the FRENCH.
(c) Battalion H.Q. to be taken over is that now occupied by 53rd R.Bde.

TABLE "B"

TRAM ACCOMMODATION.

Date.	Trams to be at:-	Time	To proceed to:-	Numbers for which accommodation required.	Change at:-	Garrison for:-	Remarks.
14.10.19.	HOLTHAUSEN.	13.00	HAAN.	170.	BENRATH and HILDEN.	Coy H.Q.) for HAAN. 1 Sect.) LOOP POST. GRÜITEN POST. ELP POST. MAHNETMUHLE POST.	
14.10.19.	HOLTHAUSEN.	13.00	HILDEN.	170.	BENRATH.	Coy H Q & 1 Sect KEMPERDICK POST. DICKHAUS POST. HILDEN STN.	
14.10.19.	HOLTHAUSEN.	13.22	HILDEN.	150.	BENRATH.	Bn. H.Q. H.Q. 2 Coys. 1½ Sections.	

TABLE "D"

MARCH TABLE.

Serial No.	Date	Unit.	From	To	Starting Point.	Time	Route	Remarks
1	15/10/19.	51st.Rifle Bde.	HILDEN.	SCHLEBUSCH.	HILDEN.	08.00	LANGENFELD - OPLADEN.	
2	"	52nd.Rifle Bde.	do.	OPLADEN.	do.	08.30	do.	
3	"	53rd.Rifle Bde.	BENRATH.	do.	BENRATH.	09.00	do.	
4	"	Brigade H.Q.	do.	do.	do.	10.00	do.	
5	"	T.M.B.	do.	do.	do.	10.10	do.	
6	"	No. 4 Coy. Train.	HILDEN.	do.	HILDEN.	09.30	do.	

WAR DIARY or INTELLIGENCE SUMMARY

Army Form C. 2118.

3rd LIGHT BRIGADE.

Place	Date	Hour	Summary of Events and Information	Remarks and references to Appendices
BENRATH,	November 1st, 1919.			
WALD,	November 2nd, 1919.	2-12	During this period the relief of the perimeter posts in the neighbourhood of BENRATH held by 51st and 52nd Battalions The Rifle Brigade was carried out by the Belgians, relief being complete on November 2nd. On the same date the 51st Bn. The Rifle Brigade relieved the Perimeter posts of the 13th Bn. The Kings Royal Rifle Corps north of GRAFRATH. On November 3rd the 52nd Bn. The Rifle Brigade relieved the perimeter posts of the 20th Bn. The Kings Royal Rifle Corps east of SOLINGEN. On completion of this relief dispositions were as follows:- 3rd Light Brigade Headquarters - WALD. 51st Bn. The Rifle Brigade - SOLINGEN, 2 Companies less 3 Platoons holding Perimeter Posts. 52nd Bn. The Rifle Brigade - SOLINGEN, 2 Companies holding Perimeter Posts. At the same time the 18th Bn. The Kings Royal Rifle Corps came under the tactical orders of the General Officer Commanding 3rd Light Brigade being located in OHLIGS.	

Army Form C. 2118.

WAR DIARY

Instructions regarding War Diaries and Intelligence Summaries are contained in F. S. Regs., Part II. and the Staff Manual respectively. Title pages will be prepared in manuscript.

(Erase heading not required.)

Summary of Events and Information

Sheet 2.

Place	Date	Hour	Summary of Events and Information	Remarks and references to Appendices
WALD.	November 2 - 12th contd.		On November 5th orders were received for a state of special readiness as Civil Disturbances were considered probable on the anniversary of the German Revolution. In order to better control the area with reduced numbers of troops available, perimeter posts were withdrawn to the neighbourhood of SOLINGEN, WALD, and OHLIGS. No great influx into the area of civilians, was however apparent and all remained quiet on November 8th, 9th and 10th.	
RIEHL BARRACKS,	November 13th & 14th.		Brigade Headquarters and 51st and 52nd Battalions the Rifle Brigade moved to RIEHL BARRACKS, COLOGNE, personnel by rail and transport by road, all perimeter posts being withdrawn. Control of SOLINGEN was taken over by the 29th Battalion The Machine Gun Corps. On arrival in COLOGNE the 3rd Light Brigade Headquarters changed its nomenclature to 2nd Rhine Garrison Brigade and came under the direct orders of RHINE GARRISON.	

Army Form C. 2118.

WAR DIARY
~~INTELLIGENCE SUMMARY.~~
(Erase heading not required.)

Instructions regarding War Diaries and Intelligence Summaries are contained in F. S. Regs., Part II. and the Staff Manual respectively. Title pages will be prepared in manuscript.

Place	Date	Hour	Summary of Events and Information	Remarks and references to Appendices
RIEHL BARRACKS,	November 13 & 14th, contd. Sheet 3.			
			The 51st Bn. The Northumberland Fusiliers joined the Brigade.	
			The 2nd Rhine Garrison Brigade was constituted as follows:-	
			51st Bn. The Northumberland Fusiliers.	
			51st Bn. The Rifle Brigade.	
			52nd Bn. The Rifle Brigade.	
			Light Trench Mortar Battery (in process of formation).	
	5/12/19.		[signature] Brigadier General, Commanding 2nd Rhine Garrison Brigade.	

www.ingramcontent.com/pod-product-compliance
Lightning Source LLC
Chambersburg PA
CBHW081428160426
43193CB00013B/2219